LITURGICAL FOUNDATIONS
OF SOCIAL POLICY IN THE
CATHOLIC AND JEWISH TRADITIONS

Liturgical Foundations
of Social Policy in the
Catholic and Jewish Traditions

DANIEL F. POLISH and
EUGENE J. FISHER, editors

UNIVERSITY OF NOTRE DAME PRESS
NOTRE DAME   LONDON

Library of Congress Cataloging in Publication Data

Main entry under title:

Liturgical foundations of social policy in the
  Catholic and Jewish traditions.

  Includes bibliographical references.
  1. Catholic Church — Liturgy — Addresses, essays,
lectures.   2. Judaism — Liturgy — Addresses, essays,
lectures.   3. Church and social problems — Catholic
Church — Addresses, essays, lectures.   4. Judaism
and social problems — Addresses, essays, lectures.
I. Polish, Daniel F.   II. Fisher, Eugene J.
BX1970.L4925   1983   264'.02   82-40378
ISBN 0-268-01267-9
ISBN 0-268-01268-7 (pbk.)

Manufactured in the United States of America

Contents

Introduction

THE IMPULSE to dialectic and to division into neat disjunctions, so characteristic of the human mind, serves to fragment the world into clearly demarcated sectors, but does a disservice to our understanding of reality. A prime example of false dichotomy is that between spirituality and social commitment. Cartographers of the religious terrain depict these, in the main, as separate and discrete territories that do not overlap and may well not even be contiguous.

Woefully, this particular map is, in too many instances, correct. Many are the pilgrims on spiritual quest who are content to remove themselves from the needs, as well as the blandishments, of the world. They narrow their focus to the more circumscribed horizon of their own spiritual welfare. They isolate themselves in their effort to be alone with their God.

At the other end of the spectrum, too often, are the champions of social action. So involved do they become in acting in the arena of the world's ills that their lifelines to the spiritual source that must nourish such endeavors become attenuated and may indeed sever. Still speaking in the name of religion, these social activists can become so enmeshed in this-worldly categories that they cease functioning as religious persons.

Spiritual persons and social activists of these types may well occupy no common ground. It seems fair to say that this pattern represents a degeneration of both spirituality and social action. Spiritual devotion that does not draw one back to the ills of the world verges on the solipsistic. At the least, it may be but another form of narcissism and preoccupation with one's own self and one's own welfare that is too much a hallmark of the times. As such, it is essentially irreligious, a paradoxically perverse form of idolatry. Religious social action sundered from the font of religious authenticity is endangered by its own superficiality. It runs the risk of being reduced to, but serving as the sacral vestments of, what is merely some secular ideology. Thus deracinated, it can easily be abused and manipulated to fundamentally irreligious ends.

Happily, the history of religion is replete with noble exceptions to this pattern of polarity. The giants of the Hebrew scriptures were consumed both by devotion to God and a concern for the welfare of their society. The literary prophets were neither seers nor social critics alone. Rather, their words of chastisement to their people burst forth as a consequence of their passionate encounter with the Divine. In our day, there have been men and women who have been forceful exponents of both the spiritual and social dimensions of religion. Abraham Joshua Heschel was one of the most compelling articulators of the spiritual wisdom of Jewish tradition. At the same time, he spoke out forcefully and courageously on issues of justice confronting American society. Martin Luther King, Jr., in the black Protestant tradition, was not merely one of the most compelling exponents of the needs of his community; his eloquence and commitment were rooted in a profound apprehension of the spiritual mother lode of that tradition. Dorothy Day and Thomas Merton, in the Catholic communion, have given expression to some of the deepest perceptions of the spiritual insights of Catholic teaching. They also devoted themselves to giving testimony to the authentic social imperatives of their faith. These men and women witnessed to true spiritual visions. They also addressed themselves earnestly to the needs of their society. They saw both faces of religion. They lived out, socially, the deepest resonances of its spiritual message.

Still, in the minds of too many persons, the realms of spirituality and social commitment remain separate and perhaps even antithetical. In response to this perception, a conference on the subject of "the expression of social justice in the Jewish and Catholic traditions" was convened in the Spring of 1980 by the Synagogue Council of America and the Secretariat for Catholic-Jewish relations of the National Conference of Catholic Bishops. This conference was held at Notre Dame University, with the cooperation of the Center for Pastoral and Social Ministry. A grant from the National Endowment for the Humanities assisted in its execution. The conference, some of the papers of which serve as the basis of the present volume, was devoted to the various modes in which the Catholic and Jewish communities express social commitment. These modes include a range of cultural forms. The papers that we have selected for inclusion here focus on liturgy.

It has been said that to truly understand a religious tradition, one should turn to its liturgy. For in the liturgy of a religious community are expressed the convictions and commitments that undergird it. Though members of a faith community might be unfamiliar with the complexities of its doctrines and the subtleties of its scriptural exegesis, they will be intimately familiar with the elements of the worship service of that community, which are woven like a crimson thread through the life of the community and the individual. The words of our liturgies are repeated with insistent regularity, through our days and throughout our days, establishing themselves in our memories and consciousnesses. The message of the vision they convey cannot but become a part of our worldviews, and cannot but express themselves in our actions in the world. If we want to properly examine what motivates authentic Jewish and Catholic social commitment, we could not do better than to turn to the liturgies, which express and shape the values of those communities.

The liturgy forms the core of the religious life of both of these two communities. It is, no less, the point at which true spirituality and authentic social concern overlap. For in liturgy is expressed the ground value that informs both of these expressions of faith. At the heart of the worship service is the experience of self-transcendence. In worship we are called out of the world of our ordinary experience and into the realm of the divine. We cannot pray if we are trapped in the narrow confines of our own mundane life. True prayer demands of us the ability to rise beyond ourselves; the expansiveness to see ourselves and our world not from our own vantage, but from God's; the capacity to care about creation not in light of expedience and self-interest, but with the empathetic concern we associate with the divine. Such attributes appropriately describe both the person who has attained spiritual fulfillment, and the person who burns with the passion for social equity.

In worship we are enabled to become *ecstatic*, to stand outside ourselves, to move beyond our normal confines and there encounter the divine. In the worship patterns of the Jewish and Catholic traditions, we are moved beyond ourselves on another plane as well. In both of these faith communities, individual prayer is not the norm. Instead, we must enter into community as a prerequisite for entering into communion with God. We are forced out of self-preoccupation into a recognition of ourselves as part of a broader reality.

As we enter community for the purpose of prayer, we have forced upon ourselves the awareness that community is the normative status of our reality. The problems and burdens of the community are not extrinsic to us, but the very stuff of our human estate. The mandate to collective worship is also a summons to concern for the collective welfare. We cannot pray in isolation, neither can we live in isolation. As we must look to others for the fulfillment of our spiritual needs, so are others entitled to look to us for the fulfillment of their needs, corporeal no less than spiritual. Community worship becomes the paradigm for community life. Awareness that we are of the community is the first step toward a sense of social responsibility.

In contrast to the charges made by religion's "cultured despisers," in prayer we divest ourselves of illusion. To enter into prayer, we must abandon the fantasy that we are the "masters of our fate, the captains of our soul." In prayer, we see ourselves instead as finite, limited, powerless over the greater forces that shape and control our lives. We confront our limitations and are forced to admit that limitation is the stamp of our creatureliness. The acceptance of this reality expresses itself in spiritual quest in terms of striving for encounter with the Creator. In social concern, it expresses itself in terms of an inherent affinity for others of God's creatures. They, no more than we, are responsible for their various estates. They, no more than we, can control what befalls them. We are, all of us, equally limited. As fellow creatures they have claim on our concern and affection. They have claim on our help to the degree that we are able to extend it. If we are truly creatures alike of the same Creator, then mutual sympathy is more than incidental to our self-understanding. If, in the language of both these traditions, we are children of God, then we must see ourselves as brothers and sisters to one another.

The liturgies of these two faith communities demand self-transcendence. They evoke the sense of community and the sense of common creatureliness that undergird both true spirituality and authentic social action. These themes are enunciated, in the Jewish tradition, with the greatest clarity in the constellation of values associated with the celebration of the Shabbat—the Sabbath, the liturgical event *par excellence*. Shabbat, in its turn, is said to be a foretaste of the world-to-come—what in Christian tradition is called the kingdom of God. That world-to-come is said to be *Yom shekulo shabbat*, a day that is wholly Shabbat. To align our study of the intersection of the liturgies of these two traditions with social commitment, we have been guided by the qualities that are said to characterize that time of which Shabbat, the liturgical event *par excellence*, is but a foretaste; that time of complete spiritual realization; that time that is the goal of all the efforts made for social improvement.

Shabbat is, above all, a time of shalom. "Shabbat shalom," with which Jews greet one another on that day, is, properly understood, more than a salutation; it is itself a prayer. Shalom means much more than simply peace. It is infused with resonances of wholeness, of harmony. Shalom as wholeness is associated with a sense of physical wholeness—of health, of the harmony of body and spirit. Shalom, similarly, calls forth the expectation of *shalom bein adam l'chavero*, wholeness between persons, harmony in the social fabric—absence of contention, and more than that, a sense of societal integrity and justice. Shabbat, as the time when we cease creating and allow ourselves to be simply creatures, implies, finally, a shalom that bespeaks harmony between humankind and its physical environment. The case studies of this volume, then, will treat of Jewish and Catholic perspectives on the issues of health, interpersonal justice, and environmental conservation.

These themes will be discussed in the light of how they are treated in our respective liturgies and how these liturgies in turn shape our attitudes toward them. This approach to these issues, still very much matters of immediate relevance in our society, rests on the belief, already expressed, that the liturgies of these two traditions are at the core of the ideological universe of each of them. Liturgy expresses values. Liturgy shapes values. True, at bottom, liturgy is the act of prayer in which our aspirations are addressed to God. Yet, we cannot avoid eavesdropping on those aspirations. And what we hear of our own words shapes our lives.

Why, it might be asked, is the liturgy — of all subjects — dealt with in this dialogical fashion? Jews and Catholics share certain things — the Hebrew scriptures; a painful, often conflictive, history of interaction; even the historical background of Jesus' teaching. But liturgy we clearly do not share. Here we are very much separate and distinct from one another. Here we clearly go each our own way.

That precisely is what motivated our selection of liturgy as the focus of this volume. One reason for pursuing this subject in collaboration is to help each community gain a deeper understanding of the realities of the other at the very point where we are most removed from, and least known to, one another. In the course of this exchange, we can each come to know something of the prayer world and the core values of our neighbors.

There is yet another reason for pursuing precisely the matter of liturgy together. As each of these two faith communities turns inward for prayer, it takes its own practices and perceptions almost for granted. It loses sight of the fact that its patterns participate in a phenomenological morphology. Each of us can see ourselves more clearly as we are reflected in the encounter with the other. In their forms and actions, we may see aspects and elements of our own that we had not previously noted or appreciated. In gaining insight into the reality of the other, we may come to comprehend ourselves more fully. We can each understand our own prayers better when attended to in the light of the prayer life of the other.

We believe that Jews and Catholics, in seeking to understand the interpenetration of spirituality and social commitments — as here essayed through the medium of liturgy — in their own tradition, will benefit from insight gained through encounter with the other. The journey represented in this volume is one of dialogical understanding. In sharing the journey, we each learn about the other and about the deepest reality of ourselves.

For the journey to be ultimately successful, it must take us to a common goal. That goal will not, itself, be liturgical. Jews and Catholics cannot share a liturgy — our theologies and our histories rebel at that. But we can work together — and this as persons of prayer, persons attuned to self-transcendence. We can translate those shared values of our respective prayer traditions into reality — a reality that transforms a world of disease, discord, and destructiveness into *Yom shekulo Shabbat*, the day that is wholly Shabbat. We can expend ourselves to bring closer the time when

> They shall not hurt nor destroy
> in all My holy mountain
> For the earth shall be full of the
>   knowledge of the Lord
> As the waters cover the sea.
>   [Isaiah 11:9]

                                        D.F.P. & E.J.F.

I. Liturgical Sources for Social Commitment

Introduction

THESE FIRST TWO PAPERS, one by a Jewish scholar, the other by a Catholic, seek to establish an initial understanding of the questions to be probed in the case studies, as well as a general orientation to the rich traditional sources that each community brings to bear on the social issues confronting all humanity. In each essay, as throughout this volume, the dynamic of presentation can be seen as twofold, at once internal and external.

Internally, the essays reflect something of the development of the traditions over the centuries as they have grappled with the question of how religion functions: should religion be primarily the response of the individual to the divine, or is it by definition communal and social in nature? Should it orient us *out* of this world, toward the divine? Or, by bringing us into contact with the transcendent implications of human living, does it perforce challenge us to *into* the world to assist in healing the world's divisions and injustices?

Externally, in the very recitation of our liturgical resources one to the other, the authors bear witness to a sense of need, a desire to grapple with common social problems — not in isolation but in concert with others also religiously motivated to the building up of the kingdom of justice and harmony in a world beset by so many potential disasters, physical as well as spiritual.

Lawrence Hoffman presents and comments on the Jewish religious cycle of worship, relating it also to the Jewish way of life as a life of engagement in and for the healing of the world.

John Gurrieri, limiting his paper to the relationship of the church's liturgical worship to the social dimensions of human living, initiates a pattern that can be discerned throughout the Catholic contributions to this volume. Although the liturgy as such can offer no specific solutions to social ills, as he sees it, in its communal aspect as the worship offered by a covenant people, liturgy can order that people toward each other and toward all specifically human concerns. The church may have de-emphasized this aspect of its liturgical life at times in the past, but the Second Vatican Council established the basis for a profound renewal of vision in this respect.

The History, Structure, and Theology of Jewish Synagogue and Home Liturgy: An Overview

LAWRENCE A. HOFFMAN

MODELS OF STUDY

NO DESCRIPTION of Jewish liturgy is possible without first determining the perspective from which it will be viewed, and, consequently, the questions that properly may be asked regarding it. Until modern times, what "liturgists" there were, were the rabbis themselves, who, from tannaitic times throughout the Middle Ages, did indeed ask questions of the prayers they said, albeit from their own unique and premodern point of view. They saw the entire corpus of Jewish tradition as existing in a homogeneous state, such that rules and traditions regarding liturgy were no different in kind from those about Sabbath observance, say, or kosher versus nonkosher food. Essentially, the only serious question to be asked was, What does God demand of me? This question could be posed regarding the life of prayer, as well as any other aspect of Jewish existence.

To this basic question could be added one more. It seems naturally to have followed from the first. That is, Why?, or How do we know? Thus, rabbinic writings of those many centuries posit lists of regulations regarding the life of prayer, along with explanations, both historical and exegetical, explaining how one might know that God in fact does demand the recital of the *Shema*ʿ twice each day; or the feet planted firmly together during the recitation of the *Tefillah*, and so on.

The historical explanations interest us more than do the exegetical. They are rooted in the remarkable fact that the same rabbis who postulated a Sinaitic origin for the Torah generally, knew better than to make such claims regarding their prayers. The liturgy, they recognized, arose out of specific historical periods, primarily in the critical spiritual vacuum left in the wake of the destruction of the second Temple, in the year 70 C.E. True, certain exegetical remarks in the Talmuds and related literature link liturgical customs to earlier worthies, including the patriarchs themselves, but these remarks occur side by side with etiologies showing remarkable historical consciousness. Prayers are regularly associated with real historical events and personalities. It is these reports that constitute the evidence for nineteenth- and twentieth-century reconstructions of liturgical origins.

In modern times, corresponding roughly to the last two hundred years, two schools of thought — philology and form criticism — have vied for the right to interpret Jewish liturgy. Both can be compared to the role they played in the study of the Bible.

Philology, particularly, posits a literary model. Much as the Bible is said by the documentary hypothesis to be analyzable into stratified literary units, so prayers, according to philology, are seen as divisible into chronologically disparate textual layers that once existed independently of each other, and have been compressed together since. Pertinent questions then become: (1) What is the *Urtext*, the original and thus primary document of a given prayer to which later accretions have been added? (2) Why and when were later strata added, so as to arrive at the prayers we have today? Similarly, as with the Bible, two thematically similar prayers are viewed as are the two accounts of creation in Genesis: it is asked which of the two is prior, and whether that one can be identified as an original text upon which the second was modeled. Beginning with Leopold Zunz (d. 1886) and continuing with Ismar Elbogen (d. 1943) and

Daniel Goldschmidt (d. 1974), to name but three of the most prominent liturgical philologists, this school has drawn many outstanding theories of liturgical development.

To this documentary or philological paradigm, Arthur Spanier (d. 1944) and, more forcefully, Joseph Heinemann (d. 1978) issued a striking objection. The latter denied the very existence of any *Urtext*, thus revealing the philological enterprise as essentially bankrupt. It was searching for an entity that never existed! The philological quest was thus obviously doomed to failure. And their philologically-based model of early rabbinic prayer life was false. Prayers had apparently not been composed by authoritative governing bodies, in single "proper" versions. Rather, Jewish liturgy was to be seen as the product of the people.

So this alternative form-critical approach posits new, answerable, questions. Its proponents view liturgy of the first several centuries C.E. as lacking in linguistic fixity. It is best characterized as freedom (*kavvanah*) within structure (*keva*ᶜ) —that is, the divine service contained a stipulated order of themes that were expressed differently by individual prayer leaders, thus producing a theoretically infinite number of spontaneous adumbrations of each rubric. Some of these survived as constituent prayers in extend rites, whereas the majority fell into disuse and can be reconstructed only in part from ancient or medieval texts that cite them.

Form critics, then, see the liturgy as essentially creative from the start. Rather than search for a presumed, but nonexistent, *Urtext*, they posit a different set of questions: they divide prayers according to style or form, and assign different forms to different institutions of the period in question, such as the law court, the synagogue, the Temple, or the academy of study. Prayers are explained by the institutional behavior that they mirror: the temple cult, say, or the reading of scripture by the geographically relevant lay group (*ma*ᶜ *amad*), which met for prayer during certain assigned weeks corresponding to the time of the communal offering in Jerusalem; or a law-court-argumentation with God.

At this juncture, it is fair to say that scholars lean toward the form-critical approach.

STRUCTURE, HISTORY, THEOLOGY

Public liturgical services are built around a core of daily prayers. These are elaborated on holy days so as to reflect the relevant festival moods.

The normal daily structure calls for three services: morning (*Shacharit*), afternoon (*Minchah*), and evening (ʿ*Arvit* or *Maʿariv*). In practice, the latter two are generally combined, just before and just after nightfall. On holy days, an additional service (*Musaf*) is appended to the morning one. On Yom Kippur (originally, on all fast days) a concluding service (*Neʿilah*) is recited.

Daily Service

The two central units, traceable as well (in some form) to pre-70 C.E., are the *Shemaʿ* (Deut. 6:4-9, 11:13-21; Num. 15:37-41) and its Blessings; and the *Tefillah*, "The Prayer" (known also as ʿ*Amidah* — the standing prayer — and *Shemoneh Esrei* — The Eighteen Benedictions).

The *Shemaʿ* known already to Josephus derives from Deuteronomy 6:7, "You shall speak of them . . . when you lie down and when you rise up," and, so, highlights morning and evening services. It has generally been seen as the essential liturgical creed. The *Shemaʿ* itself asserts the unity of God (along with a Deuteronomic theology regarding the covenantal promise of agricultural fecundity in return for Israel's constant loyalty).

Three accompanying benedictions explicate further the nature of Israel's God. The first is called the *Yotser,* and is generally taken as postulating God's role as creator. The second is known, technically, as *Birkat Hatorah* but is often referred to as ʾ*Ahavah Rabbah* or ʾ*Ahvat ʿOlam*, these being the opening words of the morning and evening versions of the prayer, respectively. It asserts the belief in God as revealer of Torah to God's people Israel. The *Shema*ʿ follows the *Birkat Hatorah*; after it the third blessing, the *Geʾulah*, is recited. It affirms God's role in history as redeemer, citing the exodus as the paradigmatic salvific event in Israel's history.

This writer would take issue only with the standard interpretation of the first blessing, the *Yotser*, seeing in it primarily the theological metaphor of the God of light, and viewing it as a celebration of the primary Hellenistic distinction between light and darkness, the major classification scheme that characterized the surrounding culture in which the liturgy had its origins. It is creation of light, not creation generally, that is applauded here, even though Judaism's insistent monotheism maintains that light's opposite — darkness — is also the work of the one God.

But even with this altered vision of the *Yotser*, the commonly held notion that the blessings of the *Shema*ʿ constitute a threefold theological affirmation of God as Creator, Revealer (of Torah)/Chooser (of Israel), and Redeemer remains intact. Moreover, the three blessings highlight the rabbinic structuring of time into three epoch-making events: universal beginning (creation); the selection of Israel at Sinai (revelation); and the ultimate end of time (redemption).

The *Tefillah* follows the *Shema*ʿ. It consists of a series of benedictions divisible into three groupings: the first three; the last three; and the middle thirteen, which function as the basic petitions of the liturgy. The decision to include these particular petitions in this order is attributed to Gamaliel II (ca. 90 C.E.). Philological studies — for example, those of Ismar Elbogen, Kaufmann Kohler, and Louis Finkelstein — have sought to go back in time beyond Gamaliel, and thus to unravel the historical circumstances that explain the formation of each benediction. Theoretically, it was hoped that a single original blessing might some day be arrived at, and Finkelstein, for example, posited just that. But Heinemann's recharacterization of classical Jewish liturgy has largely put an end to such studies.

It now appears that prior to Gamaliel II there existed many different sets of benedictions, "proto-*Tefillahs*" so to speak, varying both in the number of *Tefillah* blessings, and in their content. Those who accept the authenticity of chapter 51 of the Hebrew Ecclesiasticus consider it the earliest known example of such a proto-*Tefillah*. But Gamaliel's standardized list of topics slowly replaced the variety that typified the situation until then. In Babylonia, the petition for the messianic rebuilding of Zion was customarily said in the form of two separate benedictions, rather than one, dichotomizing the redemptive process into (first) the rebuilding of the Temple, and (second) the coming of the Messiah; so the "Eighteen Benedictions" now number nineteen in current traditionalist rites. Liberal liturgies often differ in this regard, the newest American Reform prayer book, for example, having eighteen only. The malediction against heretics—the so-called *birkat minim*—has been removed.

Though essentially petitionary, the *Tefillah* is yet as theologically relevant as the preceding *Shema'*. The first benediction ('*Avot*) asserts God's ongoing relationship with Israel from the days of the Patriarchs. (American Reform has added an explicit reference to the Matriarchs also, in keeping with its general thrust of sexual egalitarianism, asserted as early as 1845.) Their righteousness guarantees eventual messianic deliverance to their descendents (the doctrine of *zekhut 'avot*). The second (*Gevurot*) celebrates God's might, particularly God's power to resurrect the dead. The third is the *Kedushat Hashem*, or "sanctification of (God's) name," known popularly as the *Kedushah;* it affirms God's holiness. The last three blessings—'*Avodah, Hoda'ah,* and *Birkat Kohanim* (sometimes called *Birkat Shalom*)—are seen by some as derived from worship in the Temple cult. They petition a return of that cult (in messianic times), offer God thanksgiving, and pray for peace. The final prayer for peace contains the priestly benediction (Num. 7:24-26). Liberal liturgies differ here too, in that they do not envision a reinception of Temple sacrifice.

The greatest scholarly debate has revolved around the message inherent in the intermediary petitions. Some see a distinction between personal and national petitions, whereas others emphasize an overall nationalistic message. According to the most extreme statement of this latter view—its author,

Leon Liebreich, died before publishing his theory — the various benedictions all express the classic Jewish doctrine of salvation, beginning with knowledge of God, repentance, and divine forgiveness, and culminating in the ingathering of the exiles, the restoration of justice, reward for the righteous and punishment for the wicked, and Zion rebuilt under messianic rule.

Not every current liturgy includes all these classic theological statements. As noted above, Reform Jews, particularly, have modified some of these positions. But even the Orthodox communities, though unwilling to alter traditionally received wording of the prayers themselves, have nevertheless often used commentaries appended to the liturgy to moderate these ancient liturgical statements of faith in accordance with contemporary canons of belief.

Though the *Shema'* and the *Tefillah* are central, they are both introduced and followed by other rubrics.

Personal private prayer, for example, originally followed the *Shema'* and its blessings. But when Gamaliel prescribed the *Tefillah* there, private devotion had to be postponed to elsewhere in the service. Hence, our sources explicitly instruct worshipers to affix the *Tefillah* directly to the last of the blessings of the *Shema'*, without any personal prayer between them.

Exactly where this private prayer should be relocated, however, remained in dispute for some time. Some added their personal words to relevant benedictions of the *Tefillah*, so that personal petitions for someone's health, for example, would be appended to the eighth benediction, which requests healing in general. Others waited until the conclusion of the entire *Tefillah*, and only then offered personal petitions of whatever variety they chose. The latter practice eventually became normative, so that the Talmud advises worshipers to devote as much time as they wish to address their Maker in their own freely chosen words, but only after the *Tefillah* is over.

But by the eleventh century in Western Europe (*Machzor Vitry*), and to some extent in the Muslim east as early as the ninth (*Sedar Rav Amram*), this too had been fixed. Now, one particular example of private prayer, the words ascribed by the

Babli to Mar, son of Ravina (ca. 500), was mandated as ideal. Beyond that, there developed a lengthy series of fixed supplications (*Tachanun*) begging God to act graciously toward Israel, despite that people's paucity of good works. So today's liturgy appends to the *Tefillah* first the so-called private prayer of Mar, and then *Tachanun*. Liberal liturgies generally omit the *Tachanun* entirely, and return to the original practice of mandating personally chosen words of prayer in place of the text used by Mar.

On Mondays and Thursdays, a Torah reading follows the *Tachanun*. This practice is ascribed by tradition to Ezra, who is said to have selected these occasions because they were market days. The final determination of a lectionary, however, was arrived at only gradually throughout the first several Christian centuries. In Palestine there developed the normal practice of the so-called triennial cycle—that is, reading through the Torah from beginning to end every three and a half years (on the average). Babylonian Jews, on the other hand, completed the Torah in one year, and this annual cycle is followed today. The entire weekly reading, however, is recited on Sabbath morning alone. The Monday and Thursday readings consist of only the first part thereof. In addition, the first part of the following week's reading is recited on Saturday afternoon. In sum, the weekly portion is recited in part on Saturday afternoon, Monday morning, and Thursday morning; and then read completely at the next Saturday morning service.

Reform congregations allow themselves more leniency in selecting the readings. They follow the traditional lectionary, but they do not necessarily read the entire portion. Thus all congregations read from the beginning to the end of the Torah every year, but liberal Jews rarely hear every word of every reading in any given year.

The prayers surrounding the Torah reading may go back in part to the tannaitic era, but not until the eighth century C.E. do we find any description of a lengthy series of Torah-related liturgy such as we have at this point in the service today. Much has been inserted here during the centuries that followed, including a martyrology growing out of the Crusades, an invocation of blessing for the worshipers present, and announcements for the coming new moon.

Several concluding prayers now follow. Those worth special note are the 'Alenu and the Kaddish. The message of the 'Alenu (ca. 250 C.E.) combines God's sovereignty over all (universalism) and God's election of Israel (particularism). It was originally composed for the New Year, as an introduction to that instance of the blowing of the ram's horn (shofar) that celebrates God's sovereignty, but was recited also, by about 1300 C.E., at the end of each service. The Kaddish is akin to the Lord's Prayer, though the latter seems to be composed in a prayer form that typified private prayers in tannaitic times, whereas the former has been identified with the style most characteristic of institutionalized study. It was probably intended as the conclusion to a daily study session, where it followed words of consolation (the early sermon) by calling for the coming of God's kingdom. But by the eighth century it became associated with death, and in Austria, some five hundred years later, it was known expressly as a mourners' prayer. It is said as such today, though it appears elsewhere in various forms as a sort of service "punctuation," dividing rubrics from each other.

Just as the service attracted expansions after the Tefillah, so it grew in introductory material as well. Even by the second century, many people prepared for prayer with psalms, and by the ninth century (at least) this practice had grown to an entire rubric known as Pesukei Dezimrah, or Verses of Song; the Pesukei Dezimrah precede the Shema'. The essence of this rubric is Psalms 145-150, followed by a benediction known as Birkat Hashir, or Blessing of Song. These psalms are known as the Daily Hallel, and thus form one of three Hallels in the liturgy, the other two being the Great Hallel (Ps. 136) and the Egyptian Hallel (Pss. 113-118). Generally the other Hallels are featured on holidays.

But even the introductory Verses of Song now come after yet another lengthy unit known as Birkhot Hashachar, or Morning

Benedictions. This was originally meant to be home devotion, but Amram (ninth century) already includes it in the public service, and despite centuries of debate, including staunch opposition from authorities as influential as Maimonides, this remains standard practice today. *Birkhot Hashachar* is composed principally of several blessings cited in the Talmud relevant to awakening and preparing for the new day (see Ber. 60b), and study material devoted in the main to recollecting the Temple cult. In addition, several hymns and scriptural readings have crept in during the centuries. All attempts to find some governing structural principle behind the organization of this rubric have failed. Rather, we have here a blend of public and private devotion that has changed through the years. In large part, our normal order can be dated to the fourteenth century, but to this day, one finds great variation from place to place, and rite to rite.

The afternoon service (*Minchah*) consists primarily of a *Tefillah, Tachanun,* the ʿ*Alenu,* and the *Kaddish.* The evening service (ʿ*Arvit*) features the nightime *Shemaʿ* with, however, an additional blessing (*Hashkivenu*) requesting divine protection at night. There then follows a *Tefillah* that originally was optional in this service, but by the twelfth century was treated as obligatory (so, Maimonides). The service concludes with ʿ*Alenu* and *Kaddish.*

Sabbath Liturgy

The basic core outlined above is simply altered for special days, with (1) a variety of linguistic changes in standard prayers, and (2) the inclusion of new material befitting the day's theme.

In general, the Sabbath is treated as a foretaste of the perfect messianic age, so the thirteen intermediary *Tefillah* benedictions, which are petitionary in nature, and which would therefore imply a lack, or imperfection, are replaced with a single nonpetitionary benediction affirming the day's sanctity (*Kedushat Hayom*). The morning Torah reading (see above) is supplemented by a reading from the prophets (*Haftarah*). Whether this prophetic lectionary was determined at an early date depends on one's understanding of Luke 4:17. Most scholars are inclined to the opinion that this pericope does not indicate that Jesus was given a fixed portion to read, but if he was, then at least some prophetic passages may already have been fixed by the first century. In any case, by the Middle Ages, numerous *Haftarah* readings had become important enough to lend their names to the Sabbaths on which they fell, encapsulating the mood or theme of those days or seasons (for example, the Sabbath of Return, between Rosh Hashanah and Yom Kippur — see below).

At home, a locus equally as important as the synagogue for Jewish worship, one introduces the Sabbath by another *Kedushat Hayom* (Sanctification of the Day), called *Kiddush*, which accompanies the drinking of wine and the lighting of candles; these two practices date from the first century, if not earlier, though the benediction accompaning the Sabbath lights is a later addition (ninth century) and can probably be explained as a polemic against the Karaites, a sect that denied the oral law, and deliberately refrained from kindling Sabbath lights. At Sabbath's end, the *Havdalah* prayer asserts Judaism's fundamental binery division of reality into realms of sacred and profane.

There are yet two more services for the Sabbath. The first, *Musaf*, which was mentioned above, is inserted near the end of the morning (or *Shacharit*) service. It consists almost exclusively of an additional *Tefillah*, which is included in lieu of the additional offering that once characterized the cult. Reform Judaism generally omits the *Musaf* service entirely.

Since the sixteenth century, the liturgy of Friday eve has included as well a service of welcoming the Sabbath (*Kabbalat Shabbat*). This remarkable innovation is rooted in kabbalistic theosophy according to which creation is envisioned as consisting of continually advancing stages of divine emanation. The Godhead is pictured as bisexual, and the female part, or *Shekhinah*, is portrayed as the last emanation, and imagined as being in exile, so to speak, from Her male counterpart. The very existential situation of God, divided between Him- and

Her-self, thus parallels the state of our unredeemed and fragmented world. But the Sabbath, as we noted above, represents a foretaste of redemption. For the Kabbalists, this Sabbath promise meant a unification of the divine presence, pictured in vivid sexual metaphor. Accordingly, the *Kabbalat Shabbat* service provides an opportunity to welcome not only the Sabbath but, more importantly, the female aspect of God, personified as the Sabbath bride. The service progresses through the recitation of six psalms, representing the first six days of creation. The seventh day, the Sabbath, now arrives, both in fact — the service is arranged to coincide with the sunset now — and in the marking of sacred time through the liturgy. As the sun sets, the Sabbath bride is greeted with the sixteenth-century poem *Lekha Dodi* (Come my Beloved), in which the male part of God is invited to greet His feminine aspect, in preparation for divine union.

Holiday Liturgy

Like Sabbath liturgy, holiday liturgy too utilizes the principle of relevant thematic expansion of the daily set of prayers, but it differs from Sabbath worship in that it is rich in the genre of poetry known as *Piyyutim*. These are highly stylized poems conceived originally by Byzantine poets in Palestine from the fourth or fifth to the seventh centuries, and favored also as a form of cultural expression thereafter, elsewhere. No scholarly consensus exists in explaining the phenomenon, opinions ranging from seeing it as a natural creative outburst, akin to Byzantine church hymnody of the time; or, following medieval etiology, as a Jewish response to persecution. Whatever the case, of the thousands of *Piyyutim* composed through time, some have been retained in the liturgy of specifically relevant holidays.

Piyyutim are further divided according to their poetic form and the liturgical place they occupy. The most important variety (*Kerovot*) are those inserted in the *Tefillah*. But we also have insertions in the blessings of the *Shema*ᶜ, as well as other poetic forms that are built directly on the liturgical specificity of given holidays, dealing with a given holiday theme, and enlarging even further the already expanded set of prayers that marks the holiday in question. To a great extent, one can capture the mood of a holiday simply by noting the *Piyyutim* that mark its liturgy.

The pilgrimage festivals provide a good example. Biblically speaking, all three are equally rooted in the agricultural cycle. But during the tannaitic period, each attained individual uniqueness. Sukkot liturgy, naturally, focuses on the booths (*Sukkot*) and the taking of the *lulav* and the ʾ*etrog* (the "four species" commanded in Lev. 23:40). But the Tannaim extended the significance of Sukkot; the Mishnah (R.H. 1:2) associates it with judgment, and that connection is reflected in other *Piyyutim* called *Hoshanot*, which implore God to save.

Similar thematic expansion marked the rabbinic interpretation of Shavuʿot. Though originally the locus of the spring harvest, this festival came ultimately to represent the annual celebration of revelation at Sinai. So its liturgy quickly included *Piyyutim* called ʾ*Azharot*, wherein commandments are listed.

Passover, of course, is recognizable from poetic expansions relating to the exodus, and from a home *seder* ceremony with its accompanying *Haggadah* liturgy. The *Haggadah* is an independent subject in its own right, and beyond the scope of the liturgical overview offered here. Suffice it to say that the *seder* liturgy is recognizable in embryo by the first century. Its structure as we have it dates from the first and second centuries, though many traditional passages are medieval, and some reach back only a few hundred years.

The two minor festivals of Purim and Chanukah celebrate divine redemption, the former as reported in the book of Esther and the latter under the Hasmonean revolt of the second century B.C.E. These two holidays are marked liturgically by a special *Tefillah* insertion acknowledging thanksgiving "for the miracle" (ʿ*Al Hanissim*). Purim also features public liturgical recitation of the scroll of Esther, a practice paralleled, since the Middle Ages, by the reading of other scrolls as well: Lamentations on *Tishʿa Bʾav* (the day of the Temple's destruction), Ecclesiastes on Sukkot, Song of Songs on Passover, and Ruth on

Shavu'ot. The Chanukah home ritual of kindling lights for eight days contains blessings that affirm the Chanukah miracle, and derive the practice from divine command, despite the absence of supportive biblical evidence in the Hebrew canon, which lacks 1 and 2 Maccabees. Yet both blessings are talmudic (Shab. 23a), and are used by later authorities as a paradigm for the benediction on the Sabbath lights (see above).

The high holidays of Rosh Hashanah and Yom Kippur are especially noteworthy liturgically. This period represents the annual occasion for communal atonement before God, the ten days between the two holidays being expressly known as the Ten Days of Repentance, and the Sabbath falling between them as the Sabbath of Return.

Typical of Rosh Hashanah is the *shofar*, which is blown on two occasions during the day. The most important of the two is a lengthy insertion in the *Musaf Tefillah*. Structurally speaking, this added rubric is divisible into three equivalent parts. The first one affirms God's sovereignty (*Malkhuyot*); the second, God's abiding remembrance of the covenant with Israel (*Zikhronot*); and the third, the sound of the *shofar* itself (*Shofarot*), which evokes the two supreme manifestations of the covenant: Sinai and the messianic end of time. The latter two elements (*Zikhronot* and *Shofarot*) were already part of the pre-70 C.E. fast day liturgy, whereas the *Malkuyot* seems to have been added only in the second century.

Of the many Rosh Hashanah *Piyyutim*, two deserve mention. The majestic and popular *Unetaneh Tokef*, a climactic unit (*Silluk*) of a longer *Kerovah* (see above) in the *Musaf Tefillah*, affirms the beneficence of penitence, prayer, and charity in the atonement process. It should be dated to Byzantine times, despite the traditional misconception that it was born as a result of persecution in medieval Germany. The other, 'Avinu Malkenu, is a supplication for grace despite our lack of works, and derives from a brief prayer for rain by Rabbi Akiba (second century). Expanded considerably since, it now constitutes a litany that is generally said after the *Tefillah* from Rosh Hashanah to Yom Kippur.

Yom Kippur represents the climax of the penitential season,

and is accented accordingly. It begins with the famous *Kol Nidre*, an Aramaic liturgical legal formula dating from post-talmudic Palestine, but known in the vicinity of Bagdad to Natronai Gaon, in the middle of the ninth century. It is prefaced by an introduction attributed to Meir of Rothenberg (d. 1293). The *Kol Nidre* is famous, above all, for its chant that follows the oldest, or so-called *Misinai*, stratum of synagogue music, traceable to twelfth- to fifteenth-century northern Europe. Some Rosh Hashanah liturgy is included as well, notably, the *'Avinu Malkenu*; certain alterations in the *Tefillah* that emphasize the theme of being judged for the year ahead and favor the imagery of a book of life in which one is inscribed; and the *Unetaneh Tokef*.

In each service from *'Arvit* until *Ne'ilah* (see above), both a short and a long form of communal confession accompany the *Tefillah*. The concept of confession goes back to early mishnaic times where, however, it is clear that the Hebrew term *vidui* implies not only *con*fession but *pro*fession — that is, not a recognition of sin alone (as is the case today), but a coming to terms with one's entire stance before God in the light of one's covenantal obligation. Thus, for example, the *vidui*, or confession, accompanying the second tithe (M. M.S. 5:10-13) depicts a pilgrim who *pro*fesses his successful completion of all responsibility and calls on God to respond in appropriate covenantal fashion, by caring for the well-being of him and his family. But *con*fession of one's failure to live up to the covenantal terms is equally evident, particularly for Yom Kippur. A fixed formula was recited by the high priest in the Temple then (M. Yoma 3:8, 4:2, 6:2). The synagogue, however, at least until the end of the Amoraic period, preferred personal confessions spontaneously recited by individuals (for examples, see Yoma 87b). But by the ninth century, in addition to any private prayer that might still have been practiced, a standardized communal confession was also the norm.

The *Musaf* service is particularly rich, liturgically. First, it contains the *'Avodah*, a lengthy poetic composition recalling sacred history from creation to the establishment of the cult, with Aaron and his descendents as its priests. The Temple worship is then portrayed in loving detail, drawing heavily on mishnaic recollections of what transpired. *Musaf* also contains a section memorializing the dead, known as *Hazkarat Neshamot*, or, more commonly, simply as *Yizkor*. Two of the three basic prayers of this unit are derivations of the *Memorbuch* tradition of post-Crusade central Europe; the other reflects the Chmielnitzki persecutions in seventeenth-century Poland. Liberal liturgies, notably, American and British Reform, have expanded these two rubrics, so that their *'Avodah* extends sacred history up to the present and anticipates the future; and their Memorial Service includes explicit reference to events as recent as the Holocaust. (Indeed, the Holocaust [*Yom Hasho'ah*] and the subsequent birth of the modern State of Israel [*Yom Ha'atsma'ut*] have emerged in some circles as newly created holidays with their own liturgies.)

Of the home liturgy, the most significant units (Sabbath lights, *Kiddush*, and *Havdalah*; Chanukah lights; Passover seder; the *Sukkah*, and waving the *lulav* and *'etrog*) have already been mentioned. In addition, there is the regular table liturgy — blessings over diverse foods and grace after meals — which derive from first-century strata, if not earlier, but in their final form include also material from Amoraic times and beyond. Final note should be made, therefore, of the dual liturgical focus, the synagogue and the home, which have functioned since rabbinic times as replacements for the Temple.

Catholic Liturgical Sources
of Social Commitment

JOHN A. GURRIERI

A STATEMENT made by Dom Godfrey Diekmann has helped me to focus this paper on the place and role of liturgy in the formation of Catholic social teaching and on the relationship between liturgy and the social dimensions of life itself:

> . . . for some time I have been of the opinion that in the long run perhaps the single most important thing that happened at the entire Countil [Vatican II] was that, reversing the direction of well over a thousand years, liturgy did again become in fact a chief *locus theologicus.* Almost all the theological advances of subsequent documents were either expressed explicitly or implicitly in the liturgy documents.[1]

Diekmann is correct. Even a cursory reading of *Sacrosanctum Concilium*, the Constitution on the Sacred Liturgy, bears this out. The very first paragraph of the Constitution, the first major document promulgated, set the tone and agenda for succeeding sessions of the Council and influenced the content of subsequent conciliar constitutions and decrees. It states:

> It is the goal of this most sacred Council to intensify the daily growth of Catholics in Christian living; to make more responsive to the requirements of our times those Church observances which are open to adaptation; to nurture

whatever can contribute to the unity of all who believe in Christ. . . . Hence the Council has special reasons for judging it a duty to provide for the renewal and fostering of the liturgy.[2]

In that one paragraph the conciliar fathers attest to the intimate and necessary relationship between liturgy and life. They point out that the renewal of Christian life in the contemporary world, the role of the church vis-à-vis humanity, depends on strengthening the bond among Catholics — indeed, all Christians — a bond that results from a celebration of the liturgy that embodies the principle first set down by Pius X in 1903: "The primary and indispensable source of the true Christian spirit is active and intelligent participation in the liturgy."[3]

That principle was not only repeated by Vatican II, but, building on the efforts of liturgical pioneers from the time of Pius X — for example, Dom Lambert Beauduin,[4] and the historical restorations of Pius XII[5] — the conciliar fathers declared that "the liturgy is the summit toward which the activity of the Church is directed; at the same time it is the fountain from which all her power flows." And continuing with a view developed in previous paragraphs, the Constitution relates social commitment to worship: "For the goal of apostolic works is that all who are made sons of God by faith and baptism should come together to praise God in the midst of His Church. . . . The Liturgy in its turn inspires the faithful to become 'of one heart in love' when they have tasted to their full of the paschal mysteries; it prays that 'they may grasp by deed what they hold by creed.' "[6]

Thus the Council was reaffirming liturgy as a *locus theologicus*, but in a very special way. First the liturgy is a source for theological discourse, especially in dogmatic reflections on the nature of the eucharist and other sacraments. The liturgy likewise is a *locus* for christology, ecclesiology, and other theological disciplines. In other words, Prosper of Aquitaine's *ut legem credendi lex statuat supplicandi*, or *lex orandi, lex credendi*, was accorded the importance that liturgical scholars of the fifty years before the council had already seen in it.

Secondly, the liturgy is also understood to be a *locus theo-*

logicus not only in strictly speculative theology, but also, and this was new with the Council, in pastoral theology as well. In other words, there is a relationship not only between worship and theology, but also between liturgy and life. To cite Diekmann again, the Constitution on the Sacred Liturgy recovered the "liturgy as the source and center, the inspiration, of our total Christian life." He goes on to state: "Not only do I believe in *lex orandi, lex credendi*, but also in *lex orandi, lex vivendi*."[7]

The liturgy as a source for social commitment is very much an expression of the principle *lex orandi, lex credendi*, but understood in a dynamic sense. That is to say, the liturgy, comprised of texts and rites, is a lived experience of a community of men and women, converted and initiated through baptism, and always hearing the call for continued conversion. In the texts of the liturgy one discovers certain broad lines of the commitment necessary to live the gospel message. But it is in the celebration of the liturgy in an active, intelligent, and committed manner that Catholic Christians must discover the meaning of their *engagement* in the world.

Liturgical texts, in themselves, can be an unreliable barometer of the Church's teaching on social issues, and even on some doctrinal points, because the texts are products of another age in church history, often overlaid with the piety and theology of the time. Many texts have evolved and have been canonized at a time when the concerns of later periods were not even voiced. It is rather the structure of liturgy, the ensemble of ritual symbols, metaphors, rites, and texts, and the intentions of the liturgical elements that enable us to discover liturgy as a source for social commitment and for the church's teaching on social issues and policy formation. This does not imply that there are *no* liturgical texts that "teach" social doctrine, or more importantly, generate active social consciousness. In fact there are many in the newly revised liturgical books.

Therefore, the dialogue we begin on sources for social commitment from Jewish and Catholic perspectives, especially through an analysis of our respective liturgies, might best be focused by a common realization that it is more fruitful to understand lived worship in our *tradition*, rather than in the texts of worship, as the true source of our commitment as Catholics and Jews to the social needs of humanity. Further, the normal Sabbath and Sunday liturgies stem from a common source. Jews and Christians as worshiping communities are able to speak with a common voice on many social issues because they worship in a manner common to both, even if the content of our respective liturgies diverges in some fundamental areas.

Yet it is also important to be aware that even lived worship experience may not always indicate the need for social commitment on the part of worshipers. Although it is true that many men and women involved in the early years of the Catholic liturgical movement were deeply committed as well to the emerging social teaching of the church, most Catholics did not see the connection between piously attending Sunday liturgy (even daily Mass) and participating in what was then termed Catholic Action. The founding father of the liturgical movement in the United States, Dom Virgil Michel, is as well known for his book *Christian Social Reconstruction*, a commentary on *Quadragesimo Anno*, as he is for his numerous essays on liturgy.[8] Michel deplored the attitude that "the restoration of the liturgy would alone solve most modern ills," as well as the "short-sightedness which caused such false impressions. . . . Active sharing in the liturgy does not absolutely guarantee a general social mentality, even if this is often its fruit."[9] Yet for Michel and many other liturgical reformers the liturgical and social apostolates were very much united, and in a sense, formed one movement in which a people intelligently and prayerfully participating in the liturgy of the church is also a people deeply committed to a socially reconstructed world.[10]

The Lived Worship Experience and Social Commitment

The liturgy as the *lex vivendi* of the church primarily celebrates, according to the faith of the church, the mystery of

Jesus Christ as the revelation of the justice of God realized in "the unfolding of the mystery hidden from all ages, revealed in Jesus' death and resurrection, and being accomplished now in creation by his Spirit at work in the world and in the Church. Thus the liturgy celebrates and accomplishes social justice."[11] This view of the liturgy focuses on worship as the celebration, not only of the praise of God, but also of the covenant established by God with his people in the mystery of Christ as the revelation of God's loving kindness and compassionate mercy. The Sunday eucharistic celebration is the actualization through sign and symbol of what God accomplished in Jesus Christ. The passover experience of Jesus, which is at the core of each sacramental/liturgical celebration, converts and empowers the community *as community*, as well as individuals worshiping in common, to bring the *iustitia Dei* to bear on the world.

Worship is a covenant experience that presupposes and at the same time brings about conversion and reconciliation, of which the ultimate goal is communion. The structure of the eucharistic celebration demonstrates this fundamental view of Christian worship. The community gathers in joy first to hear God's word in the scriptures and in the interpretive homily. Hearing the word has several goals: the proclamation of the word is for conversion of the interior self and of the community; the word prepares also for the sacrament to be celebrated. Yet there is no dichotomy between word and sacrament, even if they are distinct realities. For the sacrament — the eucharist — is itself a proclamation of the word that comes to fruition in the communion of the worshipers with God and with one another. It is the communion that seals the covenant again and again between God and the people gathered in liturgical assembly. For this reason, the Sunday liturgy is the pivotal experience for Christians and structures their life in the day-to-day world, and provides not merely the rationale, but the very source, of Christians' response to the issues, needs, and problems of the world. For as a covenant experience, the eucharistic liturgy implies a special obligation toward creation and one's fellow human beings, a duty rooted in the central Christian mystery (the passover mystery of Christ), and celebrated liturgically —

that is, through sign and symbol. However, not only is the eucharist a celebration of what Christian faith states to be a once-for-all experience, but it is also an expression of the manner in which the worshiper is to live. The Christian must also die and rise, experience the passover of Jesus, which means living-for-others.

The three-movement liturgy of the eucharist (proclamation of the word, eucharistic prayer or anaphora, and communion) is a mirror, then, of the lifestyle the Christian is called to adopt: to listen for the word of God in life, to die to self — that is, be converted by the word — and rise to new life — that is, live in communion with others. The word of God, however, proclaims a change of heart, not for motives of ascetic self-perfection, but rather for changing the world. The truly converted person cannot accept the politics of poverty and oppression, because inequity and injustice are denials of the paschal mystery, which affirms the goodness of God's creation and the obligation of the creative stewardship of humanity, and the dignity of the human person.

For Christians of the early years of the church's history, participation in the eucharistic liturgy did not simply entail prayer, song, and other external ritual elements, but also concretized their personal role in the life of the church. Above all this meant forging a true community of rich and poor in one fellowship. The realization that there could be no service of God without service of one's brothers and sisters was very strong. Two themes converged in the eucharist: the poor (and their place in the mission of Christ) and the messianic meal. In the kingdom the poor will be gathered together and will sit down to the great banquet of the Messiah, as the prophets foretold.[12]

Thus the eucharist as covenant meal had, and still has, an eschatological dimension of social significance. The eucharist is not for the rich or for an elite, but for all people. It foreshadows the messianic kingdom and the messianic banquet. This theme is evident not only in the early history of the church, but is strongly affirmed in the Constitution on the Liturgy:

In the earthly liturgy, by way of foretaste, we share in that heavenly liturgy which is celebrated in the holy city of Jerusalem toward which we journey as pilgrims.[13]

The eschatological dimension of eucharistic liturgy underlines and reenforces the need for social commitment on the part of worshiping participants. For in the liturgy Christians discover their social nature. "If man is, by nature, in the world and in history, he is, *by nature* in society. The person exists and develops only in communities."[14] Men and women participating in the liturgy, therefore, are being formed by the liturgy. Their religious and social sensibilities are being nurtured by the liturgy, and "the human surface [face] of the liturgy is the assembly. It is in the assembly that the mystery is accomplished. The Church is a people, not an aggregate of individual salvations."[15]

The vision then of the Constitution on the Liturgy and subsequent major documents of liturgical reform — what has been called the "classical vision of the Christian experience"[16] — must be interpreted in the light of the larger perspectives and aspirations of *Gaudium et Spes*, the Constitution on the Church in the Modern World. There the Council declares that there is a way to God that human existence itself and the activities of men and women in the world offer.[17] The concerns of the Church, this people gathered to praise, glorify, and give thanks to God in liturgical celebration, are the concerns of this gathered people, this assembly. They are not the concerns of an abstract church, or even of the hierarchy only, as was once thought.[18] The social dimension of worship exists because men and women are social by nature, and because the liturgical assembly is itself the highest expression of what the church is.

SOME LITURGICAL TEXTS AND SOCIAL COMMITMENT

If the Second Vatican Council, more than fifteen years ago, felt it necessary to begin its work by promulgating the Constitution on the Sacred Liturgy before any other document or statement, it was for at least two reasons. (1) That which expresses the reality and nature of the church most deeply from an internal and external point of view is the liturgy. It is the source and summit of all the church's activity. Therefore, it had to be stated from the outset that this is so, but also that the liturgical life of the church needed a great deal of reform if the church was to be renewed. (2) The work of reform was to begin as soon as possible, with no long delays, such as occurred after the Council of Trent. The liturgical books, all of them, needed textual and structural reform: "For the liturgy is made up of unchangeable elements divinely instituted, and elements subject to change. The latter not only may but ought to be changed with the passing of time."[19]

The mandate for "a general restoration of the liturgy" did not exempt the texts of the liturgy once thought untouchable. Even the eucharistic prayer was to be revised, and several others offered. Very simply, the rationale was this: "In this restoration, both texts and rites should be drawn up so that they express more clearly the holy things they signify. Christian people . . . should be able to understand them with ease and to take part in them fully, actively, and as befits a community."[20]

Thus the social nature of the liturgy — "as befits a community" — was a major principle involved in the revision of the liturgical books, their texts and rites. And that social nature required that the books encourage full, intelligent, and active participation.

One further point involves the whole question of cultural adaptation of the liturgical books that were to appear in the vernacular. The Constitution on the Liturgy contains "Norms for Adapting the Liturgy to the Genius and Traditions of Peoples" (nn. 37-40). Although wishing to preserve "the substantial unity of the Roman Rite,"[21] the Council nevertheless did not "wish to impose a rigid uniformity in matters which do not involve the faith or the good of the whole community."[22] The ambiguity between maintaining substantial unity and not imposing rigid uniformity has by and large not been happily resolved, and is perhaps being resolved now in a manner not foreseen by the Constitution.[23]

Perhaps, as Father Seasoltz has stated:

> The idea of adaptation is inadequate to express what is involved in this issue. The Constitution on the Sacred Liturgy referred to the need for adaptation in a number of places, but the Constitution on the Church in the Modern World reflected a better understanding of the issue when it stressed the positive relationship that must exist between the Church and the world. If the liturgy is the expression of the Church's own life in the world, the cultural and social life of the world must be reflected in that liturgy. Likewise, the world must to some extent shape the life of the Church and its celebrations.[24]

Seasoltz goes on to suggest that "indigenization" is a better term. The matter of adaptation or indigenization of the liturgy and patterns of worship also needs to be placed in historical perspective:

> The liturgical reform of Vatican II was not a whim of the moment or an improvisation meant to cope with a practical need of the twentieth century. One who looks back at history realizes that Vatican II's liturgy had to come about as the result of a series of historical factors dating back as far as the eighth century. To appreciate it, one has to situate it in a historical context.[25]

Yet even when liturgical texts are found wanting either from the linguistic point of view of because of content, a liturgy cannot avoid being indigenous, for good or for ill. As David Power has said, "Cult and culture are necessarily interwoven."[26] It will perforce reflect the community that celebrates. And that is why good liturgical texts are paramount. In terms of our theme, good liturgical texts adapted to the socio-cultural milieu are necessary to affirm the social nature of liturgy and the social commitment of worshipers.

But what kind and which liturgical texts are necessary for

this task? The question of texts—their style, language, format, and content—is quite complex and is being hotly debated in this country today.[27] I do not wish to enter into that controversy. However, I think it important to distinguish between prayer texts and other texts, which are less a matter of translation than a choice or taste.

The first kind of text in the liturgy, which acts as an important source for the worshiper's social commitment, is the scriptural text itself. The three-year cycle of readings in the Sunday eucharistic celebration forms the basis for preaching and expresses both the season or feast of the day as well as the basic core mystery celebrated in every eucharist. As such the biblical texts are indispensable sources for the social dimension of worship and of the life of the worshiper. In the lessons the mystery of God's dealings with humanity is unfolded. The key to the social import of the lessons lies not only within the pericopes themselves but also in the relationship the readings have with one another by their juxtaposition. The lessons also express the liturgical season. The social dimensions of the liturgy as expressed in the readings are especially evident in the cycle of readings for the seasons of Lent and the fifty days between Easter and Pentecost. The readings of "ordinary" time perhaps best express the day-to-day ethos to which the Christian is called. Thus the readings in themselves, and as texts interpreted in the homily that weaves together "the mystery that is being celebrated and the needs of the particular community,"[28] form "the table of God's word."[29] And it is the word of God that forms the community in its ethos and social viewpoint.

The fixed and variable liturgical texts of the assembly— hymns, acclamations, psalms, antiphons—by their very nature reflect the corporate and social reality of the church. The assembly was never meant to be a passive audience, even if for several hundred years the congregation fell silent. The structure of the eucharistic liturgy demands dialogue between God and the participant, and that dialogue is effected in the communal chants, acclamations, hymns, and responses of the community. Close examination of the liturgy reveals the absence of individualistic prayers. That is, no prayer or liturgical text in the liturgy is recited or sung as the expression of individual sentiment. In fact, the General Instruction of the Roman Missal clearly states: "Any appearance of individualism or division among the faithful should be avoided, since they all are brothers in the sight of the one Father."[30] Even the presidential prayers of the priest are prayers in the name of the church, the liturgical assembly.

Every action of the assembly and every text used by the assembly has a communal purpose. The rubrics of the Roman Missal make this clear. For example, the purpose of the entrance song is not only to "open the celebration," but also to "deepen the unity of the people."[31] The rubric for the communion processional song or hymn also underlines the communal nature of both text and event: "The song during the communion of the priest and people expresses the spiritual union of the communicants who join their voices in a single song, shows the joy of all, and makes the communion procession an act of brotherhood."[32]

The sense of fellowship found in the liturgical texts used by the assembly is likewise bound up with the actions of the liturgical assembly. For example, after the liturgy of the word, members of the assembly bring forward the bread and wine to be used in the eucharist. The General Instruction of the Roman Missal relates this action to the life of the community outside the celebration: "The rite of carrying up the gifts continues the spiritual value and meaning of the ancient custom when people brought bread and wine for the liturgy from their homes. This is also the time to bring forward or to collect money or gifts for the poor and the Church."[33] The procession is accompanied by communal song precisely because this action of bringing forward gifts to the altar is not the act of the two or three individuals who perform the ritual gestures: it is the action of the whole assembly.

Thus far I have not quoted a single liturgical text in this discussion of the actions of the assembly. This is because the texts sung or recited in most of the instances mentioned — for example, communion, procession of the gifts — are *ad libitum* or unfixed. In those instances in which texts are prescribed — for example, responsories, acclamations — the corporate nature of the assembly is brought out by the mere fact of their communal recitation or singing. So, for example, the dialogue between assembly and the presiding priest that begins the eucharistic prayer:

> The Lord be with you.
> And also with you.
> Lift up your hearts.
> We lift them up to the Lord.
> Let us give thanks to the Lord our God.
> It is right to give him thanks and praise.

Or the usual response to the general intercessions in which the needs of the world and of the church are prayed for: "Lord, hear our prayer."

The presidential prayers of the priest in the liturgy, although recited or chanted by the priest alone, are always done in the name of the church — the church here and now gathered and the church throughout the world. Thus the Opening Prayer, the Prayer over the Gifts, and the Prayer after Communion and, most importantly, the eucharistic prayer are said by the priest not as an individual praying *for* others, but by an individual voicing the prayer *of* the community. The priest prays *in nomine Ecclesiae* or *in persona Ecclesiae*. Long Christian tradition also identifies the prayers of the presiding priest (or bishop) as prayers said *in persona Christi*. Christ is here understood as the Christ identified with the church, the corporate Christ, the Body of Christ that is the church.

The presidential prayers, apart from the eucharistic prayer, are of course seasonal or express some particular feast or theme. Yet the intention is always the same: to pray in the name of the community through the mediation of Christ. So, for example, the alternative Opening Prayer of the Third Sunday of Lent directs the attention of the community to the works of penance for the good of the community here and now at prayer, but also for the good of the total human community:

> God of all compassion, Father of all goodness,
> to heal the wounds our sins and selfishness bring upon us

you bid us turn to fasting, prayer, and sharing with our
brothers.

Or the words of the Prayer over the Gifts for that same Sunday:

> Lord,
> by the grace of this sacrifice
> may we who ask forgiveness
> be ready to forgive one another.

The "one another" refers not only to fellow Catholics or even
fellow Christians, but to all our brothers and sisters whom we
have sinned against.

These are but two among many possible examples in which
the corporate or social nature of sin and the corporate nature
of salvation and redemption are juxtaposed. The intention of
the Sunday's liturgy is obviously to raise the consciousness of the
assembly, as much as it is to seek forgiveness from God. Indeed
the nature of the season of Lent as a whole underscores the continued need for conversion and transformation of the individual member of the church and of the church as a human,
and therefore sinful, community. This theme is continually
echoed not only during Lent, but in most other eucharistic
liturgies. The Opening Prayer of the Fifteenth Sunday in Ordinary Time petitions God that those "who follow him [Christ]
reject what is contrary to the gospel."

One final example of presidential prayers that express the
theme of the social and corporate nature of the church — and
therefore the corporate responsibility of the church to the
world — is one of the new liturgical prayers: Eucharistic Prayer
for Masses of Reconciliation 1. This is a prayer that may be used
during the season of Lent or in other celebrations of the
eucharist in which a deeper penetration of the mystery of
reconciliation is sought. Throughout the prayer the double
theme of corporate people/corporate responsibility is woven.
The prayer opens with the praise of God and the call to "a new
and more abundant life." God is then praised for his mercy and
love: "you are always ready to forgive; we are sinners, and you
invite us to trust your mercy." The covenant is then recalled

and our sinfulness in breaking the covenant: "Time and time again we broke your covenant, but you did not abandon us. Instead, through your Son, Jesus our Lord, you bound yourself even more closely to the human family by a bond that can never be broken." Thus although it remains possible for men and women to break the covenant by their sins, the biblical theme of God's constant fidelity to the covenant is recalled. The moment when the assembly prays—the prayer goes on—is "a time of grace and reconciliation." And so: "You invite us to serve the family of mankind by opening our hearts to the fulness of your Holy Spirit." Toward the end of the prayer, in the commemorations, the prayer explicitates what reconciliation leads us to: "Help us to work together for the coming of your kingdom."

CONCLUSIONS

Throughout the liturgy of the eucharist in the Roman Catholic Church there is a continual return to some of the themes I have only touched upon: covenant, the corporate people of God, the people as sinful and as redeemed, the coming kingdom of God, and building for the kingdom. It is not of the nature of the eucharistic liturgy in its liturgical texts or as a communal action to make socio-political statements of any type whatsoever. The Christian liturgy is neither a demonstration nor a statement of socio-economic or political ideologies. Although texts will speak of the needs of the poor, of peace, and of other pressing issues, the liturgy is not as such oriented to socio-political issues.

The roots of the eucharistic liturgy are Jewish roots. The eucharist is at the same time indebted to the Temple, the synagogue, and Jewish familial piety. And as Jewish worship expresses the corporate nature of the people that is Israel, so too the eucharist is an expression of a people that believes in God who has made a covenant with it, which covenant is celebrated in a sacrifice of praise and in a messianic banquet.[34]

The liturgy is preeminently a source of Catholic social commitment for the basic reason that it is a celebration of a people. Some Christian traditions since the Reformation, and in this country particularly since the Great Awakening (and there are parallels in Catholicism),[35] give the impression that Christianity and Christian prayer are matters of individual piety. The "born again" movement reinforces this pietistical outlook in which corporate, and even individual, responsibility for the world and its people and goods is at best a marginal question in a life that is lived "only for God," whatever that may mean. The liturgy of the church denies such an outlook and seeks to strengthen, by its celebration and in its texts — praising him who needs no praise — the community as a people whose task it is to build up and prepare for the kingdom of God. Such an other-worldly outlook is founded in a healthy respect and love for this world — but only as long as "this world" is seen as but a part of, a phase in, the creation-work of the Lord who is leading men and women not to "pie in the sky," or to a better world "in the beyond," but rather to a more perfect existence whose foundations are in creation and in the handiwork of humankind.

The Lord's Prayer

In this respect, the Lord's Prayer, said by the community in every eucharistic liturgy, is paradigmatic for all Christian liturgy and for the role that liturgy plays in the deepening of Catholic social commitment. The Christian prayer *par excellence* is, in a sense, the most Jewish of our prayers. As is said so well in the Introduction to *The Lord's Prayer and Jewish Liturgy*:

> Every phrase and sentence in it evokes in a Jew's heart echoes of his own liturgical heritage and of his own fundamental religious affirmations. Christianity and Judaism are different ways to the One God. Nothing is gained spiritually by attempts to ignore or disguise the differences. But Christianity and Judaism are nourished by common roots, and certain aspects of Christianity depend on post-biblical Judaism. It is

well for both Christians and Jews to take note of that fact—
not least in a world which increasingly challenges the basic
assumptions of both Christianity and Judaism. It is well for
Christians and Jews to realize that Synagogue and Church
may not use one and the same version of what has become
the Christian prayer, but that they are certainly at one in the
affirmations underlying this prayer, and in the aspirations it
voices.[36]

I have not concentrated on the Lord's Prayer as a basis for
our dialogue on sources for social commitment. I urge all to
read the collection edited by Petuchowski and Brocke.
However, what is true of the *Oratio Dominica* is certainly true
of the spirit, intent, and much of the form of the eucharistic
liturgy in which Catholics participate Sunday after Sunday.
Worship among Catholics is or is not—and we must say this—
as much a source for our commitment to resolving social problems, problems of oppression and defamation, of war and
peace, of sickness and old age, of racism and religious bias, as
it is for those who pray in the words of the Eighteen Benedictions. In the final analysis the Lord calls us as individuals and
as peoples to a change of heart. Nowhere is this call more
powerfully made than in the experience of liturgy.

NOTES

1. Godfrey Diekmann, O.S.B., "Response: Some Memories"
(Presentation of the Berakah Award), *Worship*, 51 (July 1977), p. 369.
Geoffrey Wainwright's comprehensive study *Doxology, The Praise of
God in Worship, Doctrine and Life: A Systematic Study* (New York,
1980) is further evidence of "the liturgical way of doing theology"
(p. 1). "It is the Christian community that transmits the vision which
the theologian, as an individual human being, has seen and believed.
As a believer, the theologian is committed to serving the Christian
community in the transmission and spread of the vision among
humanity. *Worship* is the place in which that vision comes to a sharp
focus, a concentrated expression, and it is here that the vision has often
been found to be at its most appealing. The theologian's thinking
therefore properly draws on the worship of the Christian community

and is in duty bound to contribute to it" (p. 3). See David N. Power's assessment of *Doxology*, "Doxology: The Praise of God in Worship, Doctrine and Life," *Worship*, 55 (January 1981), pp. 61-69.

2. *Sacrosanctum Concilium*, The Constitution on the Sacred Liturgy, 1. The translation is that found in *The Documents of Vatican II*, Walter M. Abbot and Joseph Gallagher, eds., (America Press/ Association Press, 1966). The document is henceforth referred to as CSL.

3. As cited by Diekmann, "Response," p. 366. For the full text of Pius X's Motu Proprio *Tra le Solecitudine*, see James J. Megivern, editor, *Official Catholic Teachings: Worship and Liturgy* (Wilmington, N.C., 1978), pp. 16-26.

4. See Sonya A. Quitslund, *Beauduin: A Prophet Vindicated* (New York, 1973), and Louis Bouyer, *Dom Lambert Beauduin, un homme d'Eglise* (Paris, 1964). In the second part of his *La piété liturgigue* (Éditions de Chevetogne, 1914), Beauduin describes the *missions secondaires de la liturgie*—that is, the relationship between liturgy and the ascetical life, liturgy and prayer, liturgy and preaching, liturgy and scientific theology. Such secondary "missions" can operate fully only if the liturgy is "restored" to its most fundamental principles, and if a true liturgical piety is developed in all Christians.

5. Liturgical reform took shape during the pontificate of Pius XII, which was to prepare for the sweeping restoration of Vatican II. Especially noteworthy was Pius's encyclical letter on the liturgy *Mediator Dei* (November 30, 1947) and the various decrees that restored Holy Week and the Paschal Vigil to their proper place in the liturgical life of the church. See Megivern, *Official Catholic Teachings*, pp. 61 ff.

6. CSL 10.

7. Diekmann, "Response," p. 372. See Wainwright's considerations of the principle *lex orandi, lex credendi* in *Doxology*, pp. 218-83.

8. Virgil Michel, O.S.B., *Christian Social Reconstruction: Some Fundamentals of the Quadragesimo Anno* (Milwaukee, 1937).

9. Paul Marx, O.S.B., *Virgil Michel and the Liturgical Movement* (Collegeville, Minn., 1957), p. 412. For another appreciation of Michel's pioneering efforts in liturgical renewal, see Jeremy Hall, O.S.B., *The Full Stature of Christ: The Ecclesiology of Dom Virgil Michel* (Collegeville, Minn., 1976).

10. H. A. Reinhold, a confederate of Michel, likewise attempted to draw out the social implications of the liturgy in his many popular books on worship. So, for example, in *The Dynamics of Liturgy* (New York, 1961) Reinhold shows that individualistic pietism is foreign to

the liturgy: "Justice and charity cannot be excluded: the liturgy carried out to perfection, not only exteriorly, but even with the
knowledge and spiritual disposition striven after by the best liturgists,
will be a tinkling cymbal in the ears of God unless the ones who
celebrate it continue to glorify the same Lord in the economic, social,
political, and cultural fields" (p. 17).

11. Christopher Kiesling, "Liturgy and Social Justice," *Worship*, 51
(July 1977), p. 354. Kiesling's article is a summation of a study group's
work on the same theme at the 1977 meeting of the North American
Academy of Liturgy. See also Mark Searle, ed., *Liturgy and Social
Justice* (Collegeville, Minn., 1980), especially "The Sacrifice of
Thanksgiving and Social Justice" by Edward J. Kilmartin, S.J.

12. A. Hamman, *Vie liturgique et vie sociale* (Paris, 1968), p. 12.

13. CSL 8.

14. M.-D. Chenu, O.P., "Anthropologie de la liturgie" in *La
liturgie après Vatican II*, Unam Sanctam Collection no. 66 (Paris,
1967), p. 176.

15. Ibid.

16. J.-P. Jossua, O.P., "La Constitution 'Sacrosanctum Concilium'
dans l'ensemble de l'oeuvre conciliare," in *La liturgie après Vatican II*,
p. 149.

17. Ibid.

18. A pastoral letter of the American bishops (November 12, 1931),
prompted by the promulgation of the encyclical of Pius XI
Quadragesimo Anno, On the Reconstruction of the Social Order,
described Catholic Action as the participation of the laity in the
"labors of the hierarchy" but also cautioned "that Catholic Action is
not to be identified with political action" (*The Pastoral Letters of the
American Hierarchy, 1792-1970* [Huntington, Ind., 1971], pp.
308-9).

19. CSL 21.

20. Ibid.

21. CSL 38.

22. CSL 37.

23. The Instruction *Inaestimabile donum*, On Certain Norms Concerning Worship of the Eucharistic Mystery (April 3, 1980),
demonstrates current uneasiness with the scope of liturgical reform,
and certain contemporary trends in liturgical revival.

24. R. Kevin Seasoltz, O.S.B., *New Liturgy, New Laws* (Collegeville, Minn., 1979), p. 35.

25. Anscar J. Chupungco, C.S.B., "A Historical Survey of
Liturgical Adaptation," *Notitiae*, 174 (January 1981), p. 28. See also

Chupungco's earlier essay "Greco-Roman Culture and Liturgical Adaptation," *Notitiae*, 153 (April 1979), pp. 202-18.

26. David N. Power, O.M.I., "Cult to Culture: The Liturgical Foundation of Theology," *Worship*, 54 (November 1980), p. 483.

27. See Don E. Salier's aptly-titled article "Language in the Liturgy: Where Angels Fear to Tread," *Worship*, 52 (November 1978), pp. 482-88. In the same issue of *Worship* see Richard Toporoski, "The Language of Worship"; Daniel B. Stevick, "The Language of Prayer." See also Stevick's *Language in Worship: Reflections on a Crisis* (New York, 1970), a contribution made as the new Book of Common Prayer was being formulated by the Episcopal Church in America. Kenneth J. Larsen discusses "Language as Aural" in *Worship*, 54 (January 1980), pp. 18-35.

28. The General Instruction of the Roman Missal (GIRM) 41.

29. GIRM 34.

30. GIRM 62.

31. GIRM 25.

32. GIRM 56.

33. GIRM 49.

34. The "Jewishness" of Christian liturgical patterns has been the object of study for some time. For an introduction to the subject, see Louis Bouyer, *Eucharist: Theology and Spirituality of the Eucharistic Prayer* (Notre Dame, Ind., 1968), especially chap. 2, "Jewish Liturgy and Christian Liturgy," chap. 3, "The Word of God and the Berakah," chap. 4, "The Jewish *Berakoth*," and chap. 5, "From Jewish *Berakah* to the Christian Eucharist." Respect for the Jewish roots of Christian liturgy and for liturgical forms — e.g., the passover seder — among Christians continues to grow. See "Celebrating the Passover Seder," Bishops' Committee on the Liturgy *Newsletter* (March 1980), p. 204. For an appreciation of psalmody in Christian liturgy, see Thomas Peter Wahl, "Praying Israel's Psalms Responsibly as Christians: An Exercise in Hermeneutic," *Worship*, 54 (September 1980), pp. 386-96.

35. For such parallels see Jay P. Dolan, *Catholic Revivalism: The American Experience, 1830-1900* (Notre Dame, Ind., 1978).

36. Jakob J. Petuchowski and Michael Brocke, eds., *The Lord's Prayer and Jewish Liturgy* (New York, 1978), p. vii. The echo of passover is also to be heard in the Christian eucharist, especially in the eucharistic prayer. Symbols of salvation are found in both rituals: "How people are saved, what they are saved from and, therefore, what salvation means, are central questions in religious debate. Judaism and Christianity provide wide-ranging spectrums of possible

answers. . . . My liturgical perspective obliges me to recognize the fact that participants in a ritual are usually not conscious of the systematic theological niceties by which their experience of deliverance is defined, whereas they are conscious of the experience itself. Ritual words and actions that awaken this experience are, by definition, 'salvational' " (Lawrence A. Hoffman, "A Symbol of Salvation in the Passover Haggadah," *Worship,* 53 [November 1979], p. 519).

II. Health Care and Healing in Liturgical Expression

INTRODUCTION

IF MATERIAL DISCUSSED in later case studies on conservation and the search for justice and peace deals with large social decisions the effects of which become apparent to individuals only after rather lengthy periods of time, the issues presented in the following case study are immediate and intimately personal. How do our religious traditions frame our understanding of the human body and health? What, in our vision, is the relationship between body and spirit? How does our religious understanding of this relationship frame the practical steps our communities take toward caring for each other and institutionalizing our communal expression of that caring?

Walter Wurzburger begins by noting, as do other contributors to this volume, that Jewish ritual practice, and the beliefs that practice seeks to embody, cannot be looked upon to provide explicit guidance or specific positions on the social policy questions involved in modern health care. These involve consideration of empirical data and assessments of probability that the religious vision cannot, of itself, adjudicate.

Yet, Wurzberger continues, "immersion in God's Torah" through the study and pious observance demanded of one living a fully Jewish religious life will enable that person, in the context of the community of which he or she is a part, "to derive the insights needed to discharge our responsibilities in the world." Wurzburger proceeds to illustrate how Jewish liturgy functions "as a significant resource" for the development of values toward human life adequate to the determination of social policy in health care issues.

Both Wurzburger and Dennis Krouse spend significant time working with a question that appears to be a common problem facing Jewish and Catholic tradition alike: How can our liturgies, with their essential emphasis on reliance on God alone as ultimate Healer, at the same time provide us with motivation for becoming actively involved in caring for one another? Evidently they do, for Jews and Catholics have traditionally been extremely active in this field.

Dennis Krouse provides a contemporary context for the question, describing the approach of holistic health care and the Catholic contribution to such "integral" understandings of human health. He finds in the liturgical proclamation of the word of God a proclamation of healing that in turn impels the Christian community toward a ministry of healing considered essential to its own self-understanding. In this context he describes the aspect of healing implicit in the Catholic sacramental system, especially the rite of anointing. As with other Catholic contributors, Krouse identifies the Second Vatican Council as the turning point enabling such "worldly" and concrete, physical goals to surface more clearly in the liturgical context.

Health Care Issues
in Jewish Perspective

WALTER S. WURZBURGER

VIEWED FROM THE vantage point of a religion such as Judaism, which seeks to endow all areas of human existence with transcendent meaning and purpose, social policy questions transcend the realm of mere pragmatic utility or expediency. They represent matters of ultimate religious concern, because Jewish piety manifests itself not only in the performance of a variety of rituals, but also in the practice of loving kindness, which, according to a well-known rabbinic saying, is "the beginning and the end of the Torah."[1]

But it is one thing to affirm that religion has a vital stake in social issues, and another to spell out concretely how a religious approach affects specific positions on social policy matters. Obviously, the metaphysical and ethical attitudes engendered by a religious faith-commitment are bound to exert substantial influence on the formulation of policy. Yet it must be borne in mind that, as a general rule, decision-making policy frequently turns to considerations of empirical data, factual assessments, calculations of probability, and the like, as well as the weighing of conflicting *prima facie* moral claims. In such cases, our religious traditions are frequently unable to provide any explicit guidance whatsoever.

This holds true even with respect to many questions that arise about health care, notwithstanding the fact that the preservation of life represents one of the most basic religious imperatives. Although measured in terms of satisfaction, "One hour in the hereafter outweighs all the pleasures that one might possibly experience on earth," life in the here and now is not viewed merely as a prelude to the world-to-come.[2] On the contrary, it is intrinsically valuable because "One hour spent in repentance and good deeds in this world outweighs the entire life in the world-to-come."[3] Yet it must be realized that the doctrine of the sanctity of human life, for all its importance, can hardly provide us with any specific guidelines that would enable us to resolve delicate policy issues, such as the determination of priorities in the allocation of limited resources for health care or of the legitimacy of hazardous experimental procedures. But this reservation does not imply that the religious tradition is completely irrelevant to such issues. To begin with, the Jewish religion operates with the conviction that, in some sense, the Torah provides guidance for those seeking to fulfill God's will in the world. The adage "Turn it [i.e., the Torah] over and over because everything is contained in it"[4] reflects the belief that somehow through immersion in God's Torah we derive the insights needed to discharge our responsibilities in the world.

With Jewish piety revolving around the axis of Torah, obedience to divinely revealed legal norms constitutes the very pivot of all Jewish religious life. This, however, does not mean that all religious questions are reducible to purely legalistic terms. There are many areas that lie beyond the scope of formal, legalistic regulation. Contrary to some widespread caricatures of rabbinic Judaism, there is absolutely no justification for branding it a mere legalism. The law serves as the foundation upon which the structure of a full religious life totally dedicated to the service of God is to be erected. According to an often-cited rabbinic statement, "Jerusalem was destroyed because people were satisfied to abide by the narrow provisions of the law"[5] and completely disregarded extralegal religious imperatives.

Inasmuch as Jewish law remains silent on many aspects of social policy, a religious response to controversial social policy issues cannot possibly be provided in definitive legal categories. All one can hope for is a purely subjective religious reaction engendered by exposure to a value-system that has been formed within the matrix provided by the study and practice of Torah in the widest sense of the term. The development of a religious ethos that influences our value judgments is, in turn, conditioned by a variety of factors, such as exposure to Halakhah (Jewish law), Haggadah (nonlegal religious teachings), the influence of concrete role models, and the impact of participation in the liturgy. Because in many instances Jewish law is incapable of furnishing legally binding objective guidelines for concrete social policy issues, one must rely on purely subjective intuitive responses that somehow reflect the desire to carry out our religious mandate in the world.[6]

The reason why the liturgy can be treated as a significant resource for the development of value judgments that in turn may ultimately become constituent elements of the determination of social policy has relatively little to do with the content of the texts employed. It is rather the very act of worship and our participation in the liturgy that engenders, nourishes, or reinforces the values that ultimately come to the fore in one's stance toward social policy issues. Obviously, a prayer such as "heal us, Oh God, and we shall be healed"[7] in itself cannot yield any specific instruction regarding the extent to which society is obligated to provide adequate health care. As a matter of fact, viewed in isolation, without taking into account the normative regulations concerning the need to help the sick, the prayer might be completely misinterpreted as calling for a quietistic, *laissez-faire* approach that would leave the fate of the sick entirely in the hands of God. Because God alone is the Healer, one might conceivably infer that any form of human intervention should be regarded as an illegitimate intrusion into the divine domain. It is only when the prayer is interpreted against the background governing Jewish law that we have no choice but to interpret the meaning of the supplication for divine healing in the sense that the request for divine assistance inspires human efforts toward the promotion of physical health and well-being.

Yet notwithstanding the limitations besetting any attempt to utilize liturgical texts as a source of guidance on social policy matters, the act of worship itself constitutes an important factor in molding or reinforcing attitudes that influence the formation of social policy, especially in the area of health care. To begin with, the act of worship fulfills an important role in sensitizing human beings toward shouldering social responsibilities. In its higher forms, prayer is not an exercise in religious egotism but the opportunity to commit oneself to the service of God. Ideally, one should treat prayer not as an opportunity to submit to God an itemized list of selfish requests but rather to submit oneself to his service, in which the practice of compassion and social justice figure prominently. Indicative of the deep-rooted belief that prayer should be an integral part of the movement away from self-centeredness toward total openness to the needs of our fellow humans is the widely emulated practice of Rabbi Eleazar who prepared himself for worship by performing acts of charity, in keeping with the psalmist's prescription "in righteousness let me behold thy face" (Ps. 17:15).[8]

Prayer should be viewed as ʾ*avodah shelelev* — a sacrifice offered on the altar of the human heart. The act of worship, therefore, can play a decisive role in the transformation of an individual from egocentricity toward a theocentric existence in which the emulation of the divine moral attributes occupies a central role. It must, however, be pointed out that such a conception of worship should by no means be confused with a shallow moralism that evaluates worship solely in terms of its ensuing ethical consequences. The value of worship is intrinsic, not merely instrumental: it represents a total surrender to the service of God. By the same token, ethical actions themselves ultimately derive their significance from the fact that they are an integral part of our service to God, which mandates love of our fellow human beings. Worship, therefore, is not a means to ethics; rather, ethics constitutes a mode of worship.

It is no coincidence that Maimonides in his *Guide for the Perplexed*[9] assigned such a prominent role to prayer in the cultivation of attitudes and dispositions that mark the highest levels of intellectual and spiritual attainment. Because for Maimonides the quest for the religious ideal transcends the realm of mere obedience to divine norms, prayer performs a vital propadeutic function. The more that persons succeed in transforming themselves through emulation of the divine moral attributes, the closer they approach the ideal of *daat haShem*, knowledge of God, which is the be-all and end-all of human existence.

Although the Jewish tradition cannot furnish explicit direction on many controversial social policy issues agitating contemporary society, it leaves no doubt as to the religious significance of all efforts aiming at the protection and enhancement of human life. That preeminent religious leaders, such as Maimonides, Nachmanides, and Ritva, were practicing physicians constitutes in itself telltale evidence of the deep Jewish commitment to health care. It should also be noted that Maimonides went so far as to include hygienic measures among the religious precepts codified in his *Mishneh Torah.*[10] This, of course, is hardly surprising within the context of a religious tradition that regards the preservation of a single human life as the equivalent of the preservation of the entire universe.[11] With such commitment to the sanctity of the individual human life, we do not merely encounter stringent prohibitions against outright destruction of life through homicide or suicide, but also against any action that might prove hazardous or injurious to one's health. Characteristically, Jewish law not only proscribes such actions, but mandates positive measures geared to the protection of our physical well-being. Maimonides even codified in his *Mishneh Torah* the talmudic law that a scholar is not permitted to reside in a town where medical services are not available.[12]

Concern for health is also reflected in the important legal principle that in matters affecting one's health one must not take the kind of risks that would be permissible in situations that involve only chances of violating the ritual law.[13]

Moreover, barring three exceptions, all religious laws are suspended when they conflict with the preservation of life.[14] No individual enjoys proprietary rights over his own body; it belongs to God. Because all human life is regarded as possessing infinite value, we are not permitted to displace one life (even our own) for the sake of saving another.[15] The only exception to this rule is the case of the aggressor. One is duty-bound to resist an aggressor. If necessary, when there is no other way in which aggressors' designs can be thwarted, one must take his life, regardless as to whether one's own life or that of another innocent person is imperiled.[16]

Failure to come to the rescue of an individual whose life is endangered is regarded by the rabbinic tradition as a clear-cut violation of the biblical injunction "Thou shalt not stand idly by the blood of your fellow man."[17] Because proper care might have succeeded in prolonging a patient's life, Rabbi Akiva judges those who neglect their duty to attend to the needs of the sick as if they had violated the prohibition against shedding of blood.[18] Not only malfeasance, but also nonfeasance is treated as morally reprehensible.

There are, of course, additional grounds for why such a high priority is assigned to the visiting of the sick among the numerous activities that are classified under the general rubric of *gemilut chessadim* (performance of acts of lovingkindness)[19] or why another tannaitic source (Bava Kama 99; Exod. 18:20) interprets the verse "the way in which you shall walk" as an explicit reference to the religious commandment of visiting the sick. It is taken for granted that the presence of visitors in itself offers a measure of relief to the patient.[20] Moreover, according to the Talmud, visiting the sick provides opportunities to offer prayer in their behalf. Even on the Sabbath, when ordinarily no prayers of supplication for material needs may be offered, one indicates to the patient that it is only because of consideration for the Sabbath that one refrains from offering special prayers for his or her recovery.

It should also be noted that the Jewish liturgy provides special blessings for sick persons (explicit mentioning of the Hebrew name is desirable), at occasions when the Torah is publicly read. In cases of severe illness, family, friends, or fellow congregants frequently gather to offer special prayers for recovery. In addition, as previously mentioned, prayers for the sick are an integral part of the weekday ʿAmidah. "Heal us, Oh God, and we shall be healed, save us, and we shall be saved. Grant a perfect healing to all our wounds, for Thou are a faithful and merciful God, King and Healer."[21] It should also be noted that at this point special supplication for the recovery of a specific individual may be inserted.

Another prayer, recited daily, rhapsodizes so enthusiastically about the marvelous functioning of the human organism that it constitutes a veritable "celebration of life." God is extolled "as the Healer of all flesh, who performs wondrous deeds."[22] That the human body is capable of eliminating waste products should not be treated simply as a natural phenomenon, but as a miracle that evokes awe for the wisdom of the Creator.

It is typical of the Jewish approach to piety that concern for physical well-being expresses itself in a twofold responsibility: (1) human action (i.e., *bikur cholim*) and (2) prayers for the physical welfare of our fellow human beings. With some notable exceptions, such as when one legitimately offers prayers for death to end the suffering of a hopelessly ill patient, even though one may not perform any actions to hasten death, in most cases an end to suffering is pursued through both prayer and human action. Neither one is a substitute for the other.[23] We must act, but only God can grant success to our efforts. The very fact that one combines prayer with action reflects the dialectical tension resulting from a faith in an omnipotent God, who does not reduce human beings to puppets but wills their freedom.

Significantly, the Jewish liturgy affirms both sides of the paradox. On the one hand, it unequivocally stresses the inadequacy of all human efforts and the resulting need for exclusive dependence upon God. On the other hand, human beings are elevated to a position where they are summoned to become cocreators with God. God is not only the saving God who totally controls our destiny. He is also the commanding God who has willed that the realization of some of his purposes depend upon the free acts of human beings, who were created in his image. Hence, when human beings take the initiative in reducing pain or misery, or in enhancing human welfare, they are by no means guilty of trespassing on a domain reserved for divine action. In radical opposition to the Promethean myth, human achievement is not viewed as a challenge to divine power. On the contrary, being human entails being charged with responsibility for *yishuv ha-olom*: rendering the world more fit for human habitation.[24]

The dialectical tension between divine omnipotence and human freedom is also mirrored in the variety of approaches to health care that abound within the Jewish tradition. The phrase "Ye shall heal him" (Exod. 21:10) is interpreted by Rabbi Yishmael as an explicit sanction for the practice of medicine.[25] The fact that the Bible authorized the physician's activities indicates that human interference with normal physiological processes cannot be regarded as an unwarranted interference with or outright defiance of the divine will. In fact, Nachmanides cites this consideration as the primary reason for the need of a biblical sanction for the physician's right to engage in the practice of medicine.[26] In the absence of such a biblical warrant one might have concluded, according to Nachmanides, that because God had caused the injury, he alone should have the right to heal.

To be sure, there are some isolated opinions that restrict the applicability of the biblical license for healing to cases involving external injuries not directly caused by God; internal injuries, in this view, should be left entirely in God's hand, because he has willed the disease. This distinction, which was made by the medieval commentator Abraham Ibn Ezra, reflects an atypical pietistic stance that runs counter to the activist thrust dominating the normative mainstream of Jewish tradition. In this connection, we should recall Ibn Ezra's comment on Exodus 20:14. He interprets "Thou shalt not covet" in a radically fatalistic manner. Because God allots to all their due, it is sinful, according to Ibn Ezra, even to strive for the improvement of one's status or material welfare.

At the other end of the spectrum, we encounter the position

of Maimonides, who emphasizes that both patient and physician are duty-bound to employ or seek medical skills for therapeutic purposes. As a matter of fact, he includes the physician's obligation to heal in the overall obligation "to restore the body of one's fellow human being." For Maimonides, the case of an ailing body in principle is no different from that of a starving one. In either case, we must not remain passive or wait for miraculous divine intervention. Just as we are obliged to seek nourishment, we must seek medical help. On the other hand, the physician's obligation to treat the patient is part of the general religious obligation mandating the restoration of the body of a fellow human being.[27] Thus in contradiction to the karaitic contention that "I am the Lord thy Healer" (Exod. 16:26) shows that healing is the exclusive prerogative of God, the rabbinic tradition, as a general rule, looks upon the physician as the agent through whom the divine healing function may be exercised.

It is of course imperative that the physician be treated as the agent, not as a competitor or substitute of the divine Healer. No matter what success may be attained by human skill, it must be remembered that in the final analysis it is "God who gives the strength to perform mighty acts" (Deut. 8:18). To stress this sense of dependence on God, the rabbis ordained that prior to bloodletting—a routine medical procedure in antiquity—a special prayer be recited.[28] A number of authorities prescribe the recital of prayers before and after undergoing any form of hazardous surgery.[29] Evidently, in contradistinction to Shakespeare's exhortation in *The Tempest*, "All is lost—to prayer, to prayer," the Jew does not treat prayer as the last resort to which one turns when all else has failed. Instead, it is precisely when one employs the services of the physician that one utters the prayer that concludes with "God . . . the faithful Healer" (according to other versions, "the *gratuitous* Healer"). After recovery from illness, Jewish law prescribes that the patient express gratitude to God (B.T. *Berakhot* 54b.)

It should be noted, however, that not all authoritative opinions urge that the seeking of medical assistance is religiously mandated. According to some, though it is permissible to seek therapy, a patient ideally should forego medical treatment and look upon the illness as an opportunity for repentance, prayer, and spiritual catharsis. Advocates of this quietistic and pietistic approach tend to base themselves on the following statement of Nachmanides:

> The function of the physician is only with regard to food and drink, to admonish and instruct with regard to them. The Torah gave the physician dispensation to heal. They [i.e., the sages] did not state the Torah gave permission to be healed, rather they said since the sick has been ill and seeks to be cured, the physician should not restrain himself for they already had accustomed themselves to medical treatment. . . . When the ways of man find favor with God, he has no traffic with medical cures.[30]

It should be noted, however, that the preponderance of rabbinic opinion follows the approach of Rabbi Soloveitchik who contends that Nachmanide's advocacy of exclusive reliance on God applies only to an ideal state of affairs that has no application to current reality.[31] It should also be borne in mind that Nachmanides himself was a practicing physician.

To be sure, the Jewish tradition is by no means unappreciative of the fact that pain and suffering may play an important redemptive or cathartic role. Thus Rashi,[32] the classic medieval commentator, claims that the reason why the sages commended King Hezekiah for "concealing the Book of Cures" was that such instant cures defeated the very purpose of illness: to make the patient contrite and humble. But consideration of the spiritual benefits of suffering and pain must be balanced against the categorical demands of a religious tradition that emphasizes the obligation to reduce suffering. The tannaim went so far as to suspend the applicability of some of their enactments in cases when compliance might result in acute physical pain.[33] Moreover they stipulated that, prior to their execution, criminals be given intoxicating drinks in order to spare them any unnecessary suffering.[34] Concern for the mitigation of pain also manifests itself in a law governing the case of a *goses* (a moribund patient). To avoid undue prolonged agony, one is permitted to discontinue activities that are regarded as a hindrance to the departure of the soul.[35]

In keeping with this attitude, we encounter respected contemporary rabbinical opinions that counsel against initiating life-support measures in situations where the patient is terminally ill and the prolongation of life would cause severe pain. (Obviously only the pain of the patient and not that endured by others, such as family and friends, can be taken into consideration.) To avoid any misunderstanding, it is essential to point out that actual withdrawal of life-support equipment is an entirely different matter, for in that case human action would be directly the cause of death. Jewish law might sanction nonintervention when intervention would result only in suffering; but consideration of the sanctity of life would inevitably rule out any action that would hasten death. But in this context it is important to note that even the sanctity of life is not an absolute value; after all, there are situations where concern for the quality of life might be invoked to justify lack of intervention to prolong life. For similar reasons, most authorities would permit the administration of analgetics to the sick even though, in the long run, painkilling pills might reduce their life span.

Another indication of the extraordinary value that religious tradition assigns to medical care is the law governing acceptance of remuneration for medical services. Just as one may not receive compensation for the teaching of the Torah, or for that matter for the performance of any religious acts, one is supposed to render medical services free of charge. As noted previously, God is described in the liturgy as "gratuitous Healer." Physicians, in turn, should view their services as a sacred religious duty, for which no adequate compensation should be expected. They are, however, permitted to accept payment, if not for the services rendered, then for their time and trouble.[36]

Such attitudes are the very antithesis of some prevailing trends towards commercialization of medical health care or exploitation of patients for selfish or even scientific purposes. Health care is legitimate only to the extent that it aims at the well-being of the patient. This kind of patient-centered humanistic stance must be reflected in the approach to experimental medical or surgical procedures. No patient may be used as a guinea pig or be treated solely as a means to the advancement of science. The biblical dispensation to practice medicine is granted exclusively for the purpose of enhancing the welfare of the patient involved; hence, socio-utilitarian consideration involving the general welfare must be subordinated to the need of the individual patient.

No patient may be subjected, without informed consent, to risky experimental procedures unless there is the expectation that the patient may derive benefits from the treatment. Whether even with the informed consent of the patient high-risk experiments may be performed in cases where the patient cannot be expected to derive any benefit, is a subject of considerable disagreement among various religious authorities.[37] Moreover the sanctity of human life transcends any kind of qualitative or quantitative consideration. To discriminate against individuals on the grounds of age or socio-economic factors represents, from a religious point of view, the height of immorality.

Health care should not be evaluated in terms of an investment of societal resources designed to achieve maximal returns. Instead, it must be inspired by a religious concern for the sanctity, dignity, and infinite value of human life.

Our function is not to play God but to strive to imitate him to the best of our abilities by bringing healing to the afflicted in the same manner as we seek to emulate divine creativity by making our contribution toward *yishuv ha-olom*, the settlement of the world. Perhaps the best way to sum up Jewish attitudes toward health care would be a quotation from Yehudah HaLevi, a famous poet and theologian, who was also a practicing physician: "I do not rely on my healing. I only hope for Thy healing." With such a perspective upon its scope and function, health care ceases to be regarded as an industry; it emerges as one of the finest expressions of God-centered philanthropy — a religious vocation in the highest sense of the term.

NOTES

1. B.T. *Sotah* 14a.
2. *'Avot* 4:17.
3. Ibid.
4. Ibid.
5. B.T. *Baba Metziah* 30b.
6. For a more extensive discussion of extralegal religious responses, see my "Covenantal Imperatives," in Gersion Appel, ed., *Samuel K. Mirsky Memorial Volume*. (New York: Sura Institute, 1970), pp. 3-12.
7. ʿ*Amidah*, Daily Prayer Book.
8. B.T. *Bava Batra* 10a.
9. III, 51. For a profound treatment of the centrality of prayer, see Rabbi Joseph B. Soloveitchik, "Raayanot Al Hatefilah," *Hadarom*, vol. 4, Toshri 5739, pp. 84-106.
10. *Hilkhot* Deot, IV.
11. Mishnah *Sanhedrin* 4:5.
12. *Mishneh Torah, Hilkhot Deot*, chap. 4.
13. *Chamira Sakanta Meissura* (B.T. *Chulin* 10a).
14. B.T. *Yoma* 82a.
15. Mishnah *Ohalot*, VII: B.T. *Sanhedrin* 72b.
16. B.T. *Sanhedrin* 72b to 73a.
17. Lev. 19:16.
18. B.T. *Nedarim* 40a.
19. Maimonides, *Hilkhot Avel* 12:4.
20. B.T. *Nedarim* 39a.
21. ʿ*Amidah*, Daily Prayer Book.
22. Daily Prayer Book.
23. Rabbi Soloveitchik sees in the need to employ both human action and prayer for the recovery of the sick the paradigm to be emulated in all areas of human activity. See his "Lonely Man of Faith." *Tradition*, vol. 7, no. 2 (Summer 1965), pp. 52-53.
24. According to a rabbinic opinion, one of the reasons why a professional gambler is disqualified from giving testimony in a court of law is that he is "not engaged in *yishuv ha-olom*" (the settlement of the world): B.T. *Sanhedrin* 24b.
25. T.B. *Bava Kama* 85a.
26. Commentary to Lev. 26:11.
27. Maimonides, *Mishnah Torah, Hilkhot Nedarim* 4:4, and Commentary to Mishnah, *Nedarim* 6:8 and *Pesachim* 4:9.
28. B.T. *Barakhot* 60a.

29. See *Schulchan Arukh, Orach Chaim* 230:4.

30. Commentary to Lev. 26:11.

31. Soloveitchik, "Lonely Man," p. 53. For an opposing view, see Rabbi Abraham Karelitz, *Hazon Ish, Inyanei Emunah Ubitachon,* chap. 5.

32. B.T. *Pesachim* 56a.

33. See Immanuel Jakobovits, *Jewish Medical Ethics* (New York: Bloch, 1975), pp. 326-27.

34. *Sulchan Arukh. Yoreh Deah* 339:1.

35. B.T. *Sanhedrin* 43a.

36. *Yorah Deah* 331:2.

37. See Jakobovits, *Medical Ethics*, pp. 291-94. See also J. David Bleich, "Halakhic Ethics of Medical Practice," *Dinei Yisrael*, vol. 7, 1976, pp. 121-27.

Health and Healing
in Traditional Catholic Expression

DENNIS KROUSE

THE SUBJECT OF HEALTH and the healing process is currently a very popular one — and everyone seems to be an expert! Given the vast amount of material available on the subject and the wide popular interest, it would be easy enough to have something to say to offend everyone. Instead, I hope my reflections and cullings will be of help in our discussion and exchange of ideas, for after all is said and done, that, in my opinion, is why we are here.

In the first section of the paper I attempt to sketch what seems to me is the general context for a dialogue on Jewish and Catholic traditions regarding health and health care. Then I briefly touch upon the Catholic contribution to the history of health care. In order to understand the Catholic approach to health and healing I explore the notion of the word of God as healing, followed by a discussion of the Christian community as the context for healing and as healer. Finally, I present some questions for consideration, which I hope will spark insight, deeper reflection, and further contribution from the reader.

THE CONTEMPORARY CONTEXT

We live in a world seemingly obsessed by questions of health.

We not only talk a great deal about it, we also spend great energy and, perhaps more significantly, large sums of money in preserving or, when lost, in regaining health. The "health kick," as some call it, has become an acceptable lifestyle in America. One expects to find joggers year round in sunny California and racquet and tennis players in ubiquitous abundance. However, the "health kick" has metastasized into a "health craze": it is common to see not just a few Spartan-type joggers weathering full winter blizzards in Central Park, New York. The whole thing is beginning to smack of religious fanaticism!

I, too, must confess some submission to the new religion. I have joined an athletic club and paid the dues in one lump sum, thinking the financial expenditure the most painful part of the ordeal and best to be done quickly. I was duped! With each visit I continued to surrender my tithe in physical agony and sweaty exertion. Yet I return dutifully, convinced that my efforts to keep body and soul together will reap a just reward in the long run. But I also return because I have found an immediate and effective source of well-being and wholeness that also offers me greater physical and psychic energy. Furthermore, my masochism soothes my conscience when I enjoy an occasional dessert or glass of white wine.

These are no mean benefits, and I suspect that they have been sufficient to prod other members of a phlegmatic public into physical action: we want to be healthy. Good health enables one to enjoy loved ones, pursue a career, and experience the pleasures of life.

What is this quality of life or state of being called "health"? Exact scientific definitions are hard to come by. The World Health Organization in 1946 defined health as "a state of complete physical, mental, and social well-being and not merely the absence of disease or infirmity."[1] But this definition is criticized as "not particularly useful as an outcome measure for the evaluation of technical quality,"[2] or as one that establishes impossible goals. Daniel Callahan, director of the Hastings Institute of Society, Ethics, and the Life Sciences, recommends that the definition be replaced by something more realistic:

Health may be, most of the time, a necessary condition for well-being, but it is not a sufficient condition. By even suggesting that medicine can succeed in such a goal — which is tantamount to making medicine a keystone in the search for human happiness — there is posited for it an impossible and illusory task.[3]

Physicians are more and more aware of the dangers of any messianic claims in the practice of medicine.

In general, contemporary physicians work within the limits of diagnostic and therapeutic processes. They realize, however, that other factors are involved in the health of an individual — for example, physical and social environment, genetic make-up, lifestyle, and the quality of available medical care. Furthermore, there is the realization that much responsibility for health lies with the individual in terms of personal lifestyle and with society in terms of control of the environment.[4]

In the same way, the current popular concern for health reaches beyond the benefits of the latest jogging shoes or the medical services traditionally offered by physician, hospital, or clinic. Alternative forms of health maintenance are emerging. These forms are shaping a new understanding of health itself. Some call it revolutionary.[5] One has only to peruse the literature to discover the vast variety of tactics encompassed under the general rubric of the revolution: "holistic."[6] Malcolm Todd describes medical "holism":

[a state] in which an individual is integrated in all his levels of being: body, mind and spirit. It has been suggested that all modalities of treatment may be used in holistic healing; that is, surgery, medicine, chemotherapy, radiation, nutrition, rehabilitation, yes, hypnosis, acupuncture, psychics and, of course, religion. To achieve such a broad goal it will be necessary to tap the resources of our most learned scholars, our most sophisticated researchers, and expert commissions and practitioners. For that ultimate goal is to use these authorities to teach an individual to assume responsibility for himself and to heal himself through modification of any unhealthy attitudes, values or life styles.[7]

Todd implies two things in his statement: (1) the individual must be viewed as a harmonized whole, and (2) efforts to maintain health and to restore it when lost must also be harmonized.

The first point stresses the unity of the human person. In terms of health it tends to shift the focus away from individual ailments, their diagnosis and therapy, and to view the individual as a balanced whole. Carnegie Calian, professor of theology at the University of Dubuque, also stresses the necessity for a balance of body, mind, and spirit within the individual:

> When this triangular balance is maintained, an individual's mind, body, and spirit will relate and interact in harmony. Such a person is said to be in a healthy state. When the balance is lost and relationships are strained, illness exists even though the person in bodily terms is "healthy."[8]

The second point stresses the cooperative effort that is integral to holistic health care: "An intention of this approach is to overcome the divisions underlying the healing professions — physicians examining the body, psychiatrists and psychologists concerned with the mind, and clergy as attendants of the soul or spirit."[9] Reasonable health expectations are establishable in individual cases only when all those responsible (including of course the patient) work together. Such expectations must necessarily vary. The most practical criterion for reasonable expectation is obviously the ability of the individual to function adequately in his or her own current life situation.[10]

THE CATHOLIC CONTRIBUTION

It is precisely at the juncture of the contemporary discovery of holistic health and healing that I feel it is appropriate to introduce a discussion of the Catholic/Christian view of health and healing. This view is holistic. Joseph Sullivan makes the point well in an address to the Catholic Hospital Association: "I believe the basic reason for creating a system of Catholic health care facilities must be pastoral, based on a genuine concern for the individual's total well-being."[11] When addressing the same group a year earlier, John Quinn, archbishop of San Francisco and then president of the National Conference of Catholic Bishops, stressed that such health care is rooted in the church's vision of the human person: "The dignity of the human person is the basic principle of all Catholic social teaching." He called the defense of human dignity a "preeminent task for the Church in its teaching and its social witness."[12] This concern for the total well-being of the human person has exacted a distinct commitment from the Catholic Church of this country in terms of medical service: six hundred fifty hospitals, four hundred fifty long-term care facilities, four schools of medicine, one hundred seventy nursing schools, and numerous institutions of training in medical technology, pastoral care, and health care administration. The current record has deep roots in Catholic tradition.

During the first eight hundred years of church history the church was intimately involved with health care — primitive though it was. In the patristic period ecclesiastically recognized ranks of women (deaconesses, widows, and virgins) were often commissioned to care for the sick.[13] Monastic communities, especially in the Middle Ages, pioneered techniques in caring for the sick. In fact, monasteries were the hospitals of the day. Thomas Porath points out that the thirteenth-century prohibition against the practice of medicine by cleric or monk was contrary to a long tradition and a stance assumed by the church "simply because the practice of medicine had become 'big business' motivated more by greed than charity and because it had begun to employ methods that raised moral issues contradictory to the monastic and clerical roles."[14] The eighteenth and nineteenth centuries witnessed a great resurgence of church involvement in medical care, especially through the apostolate of religious women. During this period and subsequently, many communities of religious women were established to assist in medical care. This development coincided with the establishment of medicine itself as a professional and scientific institution. Initially religious women were not involved in health care as professionals, but rather in response to the need for humane and Christian treatment of patients. "They came as religious to bring Christian presence to the experience of illness and disability. Above all, they sought to guarantee that all patients were treated in the same way, regardless of social or economic status."[15]

The history of the Catholic involvement has reached a certain climax in recent papal teaching and in the declarations of the Second Vatican Council. Pope John XXIII (*Pacem in Terris*, 11) calls medical care a fundamental right of the human person. Pope Paul VI (*Populorum Progressio*, 12, 53) forcefully underscores the commitment of the church to medical care, especially for the poor. The entire thrust of the Constitution on the Church in the Modern World (*Gaudium et Spes*) is a challenge to the Christian community to be a leaven of healing in the world.[16]

What is it that has brought Roman Catholicism to such an extensive practical commitment to the ministry of health and healing? This fundamental question has a threefold perspective: (1) the word of God as a proclamation of healing, (2) the Christian community as the context for healing, and (3) the ministry of the church as healer.

THE WORD OF GOD AS HEALING

In recent years the understanding of the word of God among Roman Catholics has developed greatly. This theology of the word is in the first instance a rediscovery of the sense of the divine word expressed in the Hebrew scriptures and its consequent reflection in the New Testament: creation is a result of divine utterance (Gen. 1:3 ff.) and in fact reveals the creator (Ps. 19:2-5; cf. Rom. 1:19-21).[17] God's word is formative of human history: it singles out the key personalities in God's salvific plan and empowers them to shape the course of human events — for example, Abraham (Gen. 12:1-3), Moses (Exod. 3), Samuel (1 Sam. 3), and David (2 Sam. 7). God's word is prophetic: it is a living reality imparted to the prophet who in turn addresses God's people (e.g., Isa. 6:8-9; Jer. 1:9-10; Ezek.

2:9-3:3). God's word is powerful and effective of what it articulates (Isa. 55:10-11; 9; 7-9). This sense of the divine word that emerges out of a Hebrew matrix is foundational for the New Testament writers, who view the word of Jesus, and Jesus himself, as the ultimate fulfillment of that Hebrew sense.

In the synoptics Jesus' mission is imparted to him by the Father's word: "You are my beloved Son. On you my favor rests" (Mark 1:11; cf. Matt. 3:17; Luke 3:22). Jesus preaches the good news or gospel that the kingdom of God is near and calls for repentance (Mark 1:14-15; Matt. 4:12-17). In fact the synoptics, especially Luke, equate the word of God with the gospel of Jesus (Mark 2:3; Luke 5:1; 8:11; 11:28). Luke also stresses that the gospel preached by the apostles is the word of God (Acts 4:31; 6:4; 15:7).

In the Johannine corpus the word of God is not so much the gospel as it is the very utterances of Jesus: "For the one whom God has sent speaks the word of God" (John 3:34); "I solemnly assure you, the man who hears my word and has faith in him who sent me possesses eternal life" (5:24; cf. 12:47-50; 14:23). Yet the word that Jesus speaks is not his own, but that given him by the Father (8:55; 14:24; 12:49). It is in the prologue of his gospel that the Johannine author makes the highest synthesis of the person of Jesus and the word of God: "In the beginning was the Word, and the Word was in God's presence, and the Word was God. He was present to God in the beginning and apart from him nothing came to be. Whatever came to be in him, found life, life for the light of men" (1:1-4). In the fullness of time God spoke his definitive word: "The Word became flesh and made his dwelling among us" (1:14). Jesus, the creating and creative word of God, is also the word that forms history and shapes the destiny of those he calls to share in his proclamation of God's love: "I entrusted to them the message you entrusted to me and they received it" (John 17:8).

I have belabored this biblical reflection on the word because, more than a theme, the word recaptitulates and makes present the entire thrust of salvation history. As Karl Rahner notes,[18] the word manifests and effects the eschatological presence, which imparts the fullness of life. For it is the presence of the word hypostasized in Jesus that gives life (John 1:4; 10:10) and restores it (John 11:25-26, 43) — and, of significance for our purposes, effects a higher quality of life. This quality manifests the kingdom, especially through the miracles of Jesus — for example, the feeding of the multitudes and the change of water into wine at the wedding feast of Cana. These words of Jesus resonate with God's promised commitment to the life and well-being of his people made under the Mosaic covenant (Deut. 4:1; 16:20).

Life, as Jesus understood it from his own culture, was more than the mere exercise of vital functions; rather it involved fullness and the enjoyment of the pleasures of life that God himself had provided — for example, the Assyrian in promising life to Israel necessarily promises the good things of life (2 Kings 18:31-32); life is made glad with wine (Eccles. 10:19), with victory over one's enemies (Ps. 41:3; Ps. 54) and with victory over illness (Ps. 41:4; Ps. 30). Life, however, will reach its true plenitude only in the messianic time: "On this mountain the Lord of hosts will provide for all peoples a feast of rich food and choice wines, juicy, rich food and pure, choice wines. . . . He will destroy death forever. The Lord God will wipe away the tears from all faces" (Isa. 25:6-8); "Then will the eyes of the blind be opened, and the ears of the deaf be cleared; then will the lame leap like a stag, then the tongue of the dumb will sing" (Isa. 35:5-6; cf. 20:26).

Jesus proclaims that in him the messianic kingdom has dawned. In response to the question of the disciples of John the Baptizer, "Are you 'He who is to come' or are we to expect someone else?," Jesus gives this response: "Go and report to John what you have seen and heard. The blind recover their sight, cripples walk, lepers are cured, the deaf hear, dead men are raised to life, and the poor have the good news preached to them" (Luke 7:20, 22). The gospels abound with descriptions of such healings. With rich ambiguity they portray the concern and compassion of Jesus. Yet their univocal meaning is that the eschatological promises of old are being fulfilled. These healings symbolize and effect, in conjunction with Jesus' own personal victory over death, that sin and death are radically overcome for all. The New Testament holistically associates the disorder of sickness with that of sin — if not personal sin, at least original sin (Luke 13:2-5; John 9:30-34). The kingdom Jesus proclaims is one that heals all sin; in fact, sometimes his word of physical healing is coupled with his word of forgiveness (Mark 2:5, 9-12; John 5:14).

The healing power of Jesus is rooted in the dynamic of his person. Power to heal goes out from him at the mere touch of his garment (Matt. 9:20-22; 14:36). More often, however, Jesus heals simply by his word (Mark 1:23-26; Luke 17:11-16), or his word accompanied by gesture or touch (Mark 7:32; 8:22), and sometimes by touch alone (Luke 22:49). His healing is not caused but conditioned by the faith of those healed or that of their friends who bring them to Jesus (Matt 9:27-30; cf. 8:5-13); he works no miracle where faith is lacking (Matt. 13:58). All of this underscores what can be called Jesus' own "holistic" approach to those to whom he ministers.

Jesus extends his healing mission to the Twelve (Matt. 10:1), who sometimes cured by anointing with oil (Mark 6:13). The charism of healing continues in the infant church; it is recorded in the Acts of the Apostles (3:1-10; 5:15-16; 9:32-42), and listed by Paul as a recognized charism (1 Cor. 12:9). Thus by virtue of the person, example, and mandate of Jesus as the healing word of God, the church, the fellowship of his disciples, must be radically centered on and continue his ministry of healing.

The Christian Community as Context for Healing and as Healer

The church's ministry of healing is essentially related to its ministry of proclaiming the word of God in preparation for the Lord until he returns. As in the ministry of Jesus, the church's healing ministry manifests the dawning of the kingdom, a kingdom whose full coming we not only pray for daily, but must work for daily. The God of Jesus is not a pushover God, or a handout God, but a God who asks the response of full participation in the building of the kingdom. The church's commitment to this participation has been and continues to be exercised on three levels: (1) the level of charity — by establishment of institutions for primary health care (hospitals and other direct patient care facilities) and for secondary health care (medical schools, other health education programs, etc.); (2) the level of thaumaturgy — by sometimes effecting physical and psychological cures without ordinary medical intervention; and (3) the level of sacramental and pastoral care — by celebration of the sacraments, especially the anointing of the sick, and the spiritual care of the sick and dying.

In a certain sense all three levels of ministry merge and often in practice become indistinguishable. This is to be expected if we accept the principle of holistic healing and the concept that the whole person must be involved in the process of health evaluation. Nevertheless, distinctions are necessary, not only due to the cerebral propensities of theologians, but for a fuller and more precise understanding of the church's responsibility to the sick and how best to fulfill the gospel mandate to heal.

Furthermore, when confusion of these distinctions has prevailed, the role of religion in the healing process is often reduced to superstition or even charlatanism, or expanded beyond its limits to the denigration of scientific medical care.

Although all three levels of healing ministry have been exercised in the Christian community since its foundation, they have received different emphases at different periods of history.[19] The varying degree of the charitable level of healing ministry has already been mentioned. What remains for discussion here are the levels of thaumaturgic and sacramental/pastoral ministry. This is no mean task. To unravel the origins of these ministries is a formidable undertaking well beyond the intent and scope of this paper. A few observations must suffice.

As we have seen in the discussion of the word of God as healing, the understanding of health and healing for the Christian must be rooted in the person of the risen Christ. Furthermore, for this understanding to be authentic, it must flow into a sense of communal discipleship to Jesus as Lord: the community by its life of service and prayer, especially in liturgical celebration, once again makes present the Lord who is healer.[20] From the earliest times both charismatic/miraculous healing and sacramental/pastoral ministry to the sick have been intertwined and often confounded. No doubt each was looked upon as a refraction of the one unique presence of Christ the physician. Christ's concern was for human wholeness in all dimensions of life. He promised charism (Mark 16:15-20), but did not give us leave to presume the kingdom had come in its fullness. As Thomas Talley remarks on the intervention of charismatic healing:

> [It] is not covenanted, nor is it patient of liturgical institutionalization. It is by the nature of the case under consideration, the exception to every pattern, truly a wonder, a miracle. . . . Sacramental continuity and charismatic discontinuity should vitalize each other in interaction, as the priests and prophets of the Old Covenant, for without this the liturgy reverts to the law. Of the charism of healing there is in fact little to be said systematically, for it is not a systematic phenomenon.[21]

Although not much can be said systematically about thaumaturgic healing, much has been chronicled historically and in terms of contemporary renewed interest, especially among Christians of the charismatic movement.[22] In both cases the tendency is often to see "everything as a miracle," when in fact we are dealing most frequently with secondary causality and many unknown factors operative in the dialogue of medicine with the life process. On the other side, of course, are the skeptics who wag their heads, insisting that there is a scientific answer for everything. Somewhat akin are those Christian writers who seem to limit the thaumaturgic to polemics.[23]

The sacramental and pastoral level of the Christian healing ministry can be called an outgrowth of Christ's concern for the well-being of the whole person. Plato's dictum, to live alone one must either be insane or a god, applies no less to the sick than it does to the healthy of the community. Insanity is a sickness that cries out for healing, and although *theosis* is an honored, traditional teaching of the church fathers, the working of grace in our divinization is not yet complete, and even if it were, it would not preclude the necessity of community. If the triune community within the Godhead is fundamental Christian belief, no less fundamental is the belief that the person achieves highest individuation and significance only in and through a relationship with the community of believers that Christians call the Body of Christ. Sacraments, then, are not only acts of Christ, but of the whole church in harmonious concert with the Spirit who refreshes, consoles, and heals.[24] It is for this reason of paramount significance that in its liturgical revisions the Second Vatican Council stressed the full participation of the community.[25] This fundamental requirement was built into the reform of each sacrament so that the faithful can have complete access to the "primary and indispensable source of the true Christian spirit."[26]

Christian initiation, which incorporates a person into the mystery of discipleship in the Body of Christ, is a rebirthing experience that is healing to its core. The restored catechumenate, as a process of integration into the community, is healing in its prayers of exorcism and in the mutual challenge to faith that it issues between catechumen and community.

The sacrament of reconciliation as a second baptism is an experience of healing from sin and its damage to penitent and community. It is significant that the rite again normalizes communal celebrations in which the prayer and support of the community are directed to the healing of sin within its bond.

The sacramental celebration of the eucharist, being the highest liturgical expression of the paschal mystery, is the preeminent healing experience of the Christian. It is here that the full, saving presence of the risen Lord is effected and sacramentally manifested. Through it the Christian community is empowered to live life in response to the call to share the healing mission of Jesus. Often postcommunion prayers express the theme of healing.[27] The Christian mystical tradition frequently alludes to the healing nature of the eucharist, especially in the reception of communion.[28] Today eucharistic celebrations for the sick, even in homes and hospitals, are strongly encouraged; the celebration of anointing often occurs in the context of the Mass.

In the most specific way the Rite of Anointing and Pastoral Care of the Sick ministers the concern of the church for those who are shattered by the disorder of sickness and isolated by its restrictions. The celebration is an anamnesis of the dead and risen Christ who is made present and offered in the life and suffering of the sick. The church enshrines this celebration in the overarching work of pastoral visitation to the sick, which extends beyond the clerical. The whole community is invited to pray for the sick and is personified in the ministry of those who directly serve them: priest, deacon, eucharistic minister, and those who practice the corporal works of mercy, including, I might add, medical personnel.

The classic biblical text for the actual sacrament of the sick, in urging the sick to call upon the leaders of the community to pray and anoint them, is concerned with more than bodily healing and forgiveness of sin:

> Is there anyone sick among you? He should ask for the presbyters of the church. They in turn are to pray over him, anointing him with oil in the Name [of the Lord]. This prayer uttered in faith will reclaim the one who is ill, and the Lord will restore him to health. If he has committed any sins, forgiveness will be his [James 5:13-15].

Some clarification is needed for the word "reclaim" (*sosei*). It is used in the gospels in the cure of the hemorrhaging woman, implying a restoration to the community after the exclusion imposed by ritual impurity (Matt. 9:20). The word "restore" (*egerei*) often means to raise or resurrect from sleep or death. However, such an exclusively eschatological meaning does not fit the context here. Rather, the sense of healing and wholeness is implied. For example, the word is used in the cure of the paralytic (Matt. 9:6) in the context of forgiveness of sin as well as physical heaing. Likewise, when it is used in recounting the cure of Peter's mother-in-law (Mark 2:31), it implies that she is able to function in her life situation: "She immediately began waiting on them."

In his now classic article on the sacrament, Paul Palmer set the stage for the understanding of the sacrament as expressed in the renewal of Vatican II.[29] Through a careful analysis of Christian tradition he was able to dismiss the medieval notion that the sacrament was limited to an "extreme unction" and an immediate preparation for glory, and only in some remote way concerned with physical healing. Scholastic theologians, until modern times, haggled over the precise hierarchy of effects of the sacrament, but in any case concentrated almost exclusively on a narrowly interpreted spiritual side of the matter.

In recent years there has been more emphasis given to the physical implications of the sacrament's effectiveness. As we have seen, some have taken this to an extreme opposite of the medieval understanding, even to the point of attempting to institutionalize the charismatic. The balanced view proposed by the church is best expressed in the *praenotanda* of the ritual for anointing.[30] This explanation inserts the sacrament squarely into the context of Christian concern for the well-being of the whole person. The risen Christ is present to the sick person to assist in living out faithful discipleship in the face of the current life situation and to function well in that situation. Thus, the sacrament can be a preparation for glory, if, as a matter of fact, the earthly life of the person is to end, or conversely, it can be a restoration to normal living and to the community, or it can be the strength to live a life of redemptive suffering in union with the passion of Jesus. Anointing, as a sacrament, is in the genre of sign; as such, it proclaims and manifests a hidden reality — in this case the presence of the Lord who is victorious over sin and sickness, and who comes to bring life and concern for the total well-being of the sick person, who, at the same time, has not a lasting home here.

A last remark on the sacramental ministry to the sick is in order. The historical development of the praxis of anointing is as convoluted as its theology. We are only now emerging from a viewpoint that assigned it exclusively to the moribund. However, in the patristic period it is clear that the oil was imparted for the total well-being of the faithful. The earliest church orders or pastoral manuals record blessings for foodstuffs that almost always included a special prayer for oil, a household food staple as well as a medicinal panacea. Hippolytus of Rome (ca. 215) offers a model blessing for oil: "That sanctifying this oil, O God, wherewith thou didst anoint kings, priests, and prophets, thou wouldst grant health to them who use it and partake of it, so that it may bestow comfort on all who taste it and health on all who use it."[31] A certain messianic implication seems to be present in the initial part of the prayer. Eventually these prayers are considered consecratory and effective in themselves of the sacrament, in a way somewhat analogous to the understanding of the eucharistic prayer as consecratory of bread and wine. The faithful were encouraged to take the oil home to drink it or be anointed with it in the case of sickness.

Little is in evidence to support the precise distinction of scholastic theology between sacrament and sacramental. The most famous allusion to this practice is in a letter of Pope Innocent I to Bishop Decentius in 416. After quoting James 5:14-15, the pontiff states that not only priest but also faithful may anoint with oil.[32] This practice continued until the Carolingian reform with its greater stress on and definition of the role of the clergy. Perhaps this should give us greater impetus to broaden our understanding of the sacrament to a complex of rites contextualized in an ongoing pastoral care of the whole community for the sick. It begins with the first contact with the sick person, continues with regular visitation, prayer, and eucharistic communion, climaxes with the celebration of the anointing itself, and is perfected in the only way any sacrament is perfected: with the full advent of the kingdom.

THE CHALLENGES OF DIALOGUE

What are the implications of the Catholic tradition of health and healing for the specific task of this Jewish-Catholic dialogue on social policy? I think there are many. I will suggest a few in the form of questions. I hope they will serve as catalysts for the real contribution of dialogue, which is in the active give-and-take of discussion and the challenge for growth that it generates.

(1) Our traditions are rooted in a belief that the human person is made in the image and likeness of God who wills his people health and wholeness. What are the specific areas of agreement and disagreement on the question of the responsibility of our religious communities in health care?

(2) The whole person — body, mind, and spirit — must be the object of health care. How can our communities alert their memberships to this concern? Are there ways in which we can cooperate in the health education effort?

(3) Often the dignity of the human person is overshadowed by the monoliths of government and "big business" in health care. In what ways can we cooperate to combat such impersonalism, which is itself destructive of full human health?[33]

(4) Can we agree that every human being, despite economic status, has a right to medical care?[34] If so, what should be our position regarding a comprehensive national health policy? In what ways as religious groups have we hindered the exercise of this right in the world community? What are some practical steps we can take to support the universal right to health care?

(5) In view of the escalating cost of medical care and the decline of hospitals in impoverished areas, some Catholic and Protestant health care facilities have merged in this country.[35] Do our communities sufficiently share moral values and a view of health and healing so that such mergers could be feasible between Jewish and Catholic health facilities?

(6) Self-care orientation and "consumer participation" is advocated by a holistic approach to health and healing. In what mutually cooperative ways can we support these goals in practice?

(7) Alternatives to current health care facilities — such as holistic health centers, hospices, home birth — are emerging today. What responsibility do our religious communities have to assist membership in discerning the correct form of health care for their needs? Are there specific alternatives that we should actively support?

(8) The role of the clergy is being increasingly recognized in health care. Are there ways the clergy of our institutions can

cooperate in securing better access to and pastoral care of the sick?

The tasks ahead of us are gargantuan. Both of our traditions are the inheritors of a promise, which is at the same time a challenge: dignity and wholeness of life for each human person. May God give us the strength to accept the challenge and accomplish his will. May his reign come!

NOTES

1. Quoted by David B. Smith and Arnold D. Kaluzny, *The White Labyrinth: Understanding the Organization of Health Care* (Berkeley, Cal.: McCutchan, 1975) p.229. See also the discussion by Daniel Callahan, "Health and Society: Some Ethical Imperatives," *Daedalus* (Winter 1977), pp. 25-26.

2. Smith and Kaluzny, *White Labyrinth*, p. 229.

3. Callahan, "Health and Society," p. 26.

4. Malcolm C. Todd, M.D., past president of the American Medical Association (1975) makes the point trenchantly when speaking of health education: "Dangerous and apparently illogical health behavior appears as such only from the detached, rational scientific view the health professional assumes when he judges the health behavior of others. Such behavior may appear logical and necessary when viewed from inside the consumer's world. In addition, much counterproductive and dangerous health behavior is created and sustained by our society's values. Overwork, overeating, self-medication, cigarette smoking, alcohol abuse, the lack of exercise, all are examples. It is not likely that such ingrained and culturally reinforced behavior patterns can be changed solely through short-term crisis health education programs. Health education needs to be permanently integrated throughout society in a manner that will shape healthful life styles in the American people. Health education is a long term goal, not a short term panacea" "The Need for a Holistic Approach in Medicine," *Journal of Holistic Health* [San Diego: Association for Holistic Health, 1977] p. 9).

5. E.g., Harold H. Bloomfield, M.D., and Robert B. Kory, *The Holistic Way to Health and Happiness* (New York: Simon and Schuster, 1978) p. 45.

6. Ibid., passim. See also Leslie J. Kaslov, *Wholistic Dimensions in Healing: A Resource Guide* (Garden City, N.Y.: Doubleday, 1978); Kaslov's work offers a brief description of each of the principal "modalities or techniques" of holistic healing with comprehensive bibliography and information regarding resource centers and personnel.

7. Todd, "The Need for a Holistic Approach," p. 8. He also issues a *caveat* to the movement: "Be sure that it is fundamentally sound, sophisticated and generated by accepted authorities. Don't let it become a mecca for the charlatan, the faddist or the opportunist. But rather let it move in an orderly, progressive and cautious manner so as to play a vital role in our health oriented society of the twenty-first century" (p. 10).

8. Carnegie Samuel Calian, "Theological and Scientific Understandings of Health," *Hospital Progress*, 59 (Dec. 1978), p. 61.

9. Ibid.

10. See the discussion of evaluating medical effectiveness in Smith and Kaluzny, *White Labyrinth*, pp. 222-26; also helpful are the observations of Hans Schaefer, "Health, Physical," *Sacramentum Mundi*, Karl Rahner, ed. 3 (1969), pp. 3-5.

11. Joseph M. Sullivan, "Why Create a System of Catholic Health Care Facilities?," *Hospital Progress*, 57 (Sept. 1976). p. 81. See also James A. O'Donohoe, "Healing for Wholeness: The Witness of Our Catholic Care Facilities," *Linacre Quarterly*, 44 (1977), pp. 136-45. O'Donohoe describes the identity of Catholic health care as follows: "By concerning itself with those who suffer from illness, the Catholic health facility participates intimately in the healing mission of the Christian/Catholic Church. As such it must appear to all mankind as a visible sign of the healing power of Jesus who, by the gift of Himself unto death, brought order and health (salvation) into a world where disorder and sickness reigned because of human sinfulness. To be a credible sign of such a noble undertaking, the Catholic health care facility must make manifest in word and deed those three elements envisioned by contemporary society as constitutive of any religious faith: 1) a profound respect for and confidence in the Transcendent; 2) sincere action for the betterment of the human condition; 3) an unmitigated concern for building a community of justice and love" (pp. 138-39).

12. John R. Quinn, "The Public Debate on Social Justice and Health Care: An Opportunity for Evangelization," *Hospital Progress*, 60 (Aug. 1979), p. 44.

13. E.g., *Didascalia Apostolorum*, XVI, iii, 12, R. Hugh Conolly, ed. (Oxford: Clarendon Press, 1929), pp. 146-48.

14. Thomas J. Porath, "A Catholic Health Care System: Who's Responsible?," *Hospital Progress*, 60 (April 1979), p. 60. Porath gives a fine chart of the history of Catholic involvement in health care, p. 62.

15. Ibid., p. 60.

16. For a treatment of this challenge see Cornelius J. van der Poel, "Healing Mission of the Church — A Search for Human Wholeness," *Hospital Progress*, 57 (Sept. 1976), pp. 84-88. In all honesty, however, I must indicate that despite vast practical commitment to health care in the church, largely under the auspices of religious women, there is little in official Catholic documents that specifically relates to health care outside the sacramental. These documents are almost exclusively composed by male scholars, by tradition highly trained in speculative theology, and therefore less likely to be sensitive to the practical needs of the body in health care situations.

17. See Karl Rahner, "What is a Sacrament?," *Worship*, 47 (1973), p. 275.

18. There is no point here in an exhaustive presentation or analysis of these pericopes. The standard commentaries and biblical dictionaries are generally sufficient.

19. See the comprehensive discussion of this by Morton T. Kelsey, *Healing and Christianity* (New York: Harper and Row, 1973) pp. 52-103, especially pp. 81, 92-97.

20. "Christ is always present in his Church, especially in her liturgical celebrations. . . . From this it follows that every liturgical celebration, because it is an action of Christ the Priest and of his Body, which is the Church, is a sacred action surpassing all others" (Constitution on the Sacred Liturgy, 7), *Vatican Council II: The Conciliar and Post Conciliar Documents*, Austin Flannery, ed.(Collegeville, Minn.: Liturgical Press, 1975).

21. Thomas Talley, "Healing: Sacrament or Charism," *Worship*, 46 (1972), pp. 519, 527.

22. Kelsey (pp. 135-242) records this history comprehensively, even though he is at times guilty of confusing the levels of health ministry in the church, nor is he sufficiently sensitive to the distinctions between miracles strictly speaking, the power of suggestion, and the normal healing process. For another charismatically oriented approach, see Francis McNutt, *Healing* (Notre Dame, Ind.: Ave Maria Press, 1974) and *Power to Heal* (Notre Dame, Ind.: Ave Maria Press, 1977).

For a development of the theme of healing in the history of Christian ministry in the sacramental and pastoral sense, see Bernard Cooke, *Ministry to Word and Sacraments: History and Theology* (Philadelphia: Fortress Press, 1976), pp. 94-95, 212-13, 257, 400.

23. Louis Mondens, *Signs and Wonders: A Study of the Miraculous Element in Religion* (New York: Desclee, 1966); his efforts to expose the spurious are laudable, but without sufficient data he proposes to reduce all true miracles to the Roman Catholic Church; see chap. 3, "The Absence of Major Miracles Outside the Catholic Church." The area of the scientific study of miraculous healings might well be one for serious cooperation between Jewish and Catholic institutions.

24. See the Pentecost sequence, *Veni, Sancte Spiritus.*

25. Constitution on the Sacred Liturgy, 14.

26. Ibid.

27. E.g., see the postcommunion prayers for the Tenth and the Twenty-First Sundays in Ordinary Time, and for Trinity Sunday.

28. Theresa of Avila writes when speaking of both bodily and spiritual trials: "Sometimes — almost habitually, indeed, or at least very frequently — I would find relief after communicating. There were times, in fact, when the very act of approaching the Sacrament would at once make me feel so well, both in soul and in body, that I was astounded" (chap. 30) (*The Autobiography of St. Theresa of Avila,* E. Allison Peers, trans. and ed., [Garden City, N.Y.: Image Books, 1960], p. 283).

29. Paul F. Palmer, "The Purpose of Anointing the Sick: A Reappraisal," *Theological Studies,* 19 (1958), pp. 309-44; see especially pp. 312-14.

30. "The sacrament of anointing prolongs the concern which the Lord himself showed for the bodily and spiritual welfare of the sick, as the gospels testify, and which he asked his followers to show also. . . .

The one who is seriously ill needs the special help of God's grace in this time of anxiety, lest he or she be broken in spirit and subject to temptations and the weakening of faith.

Christ, therefore, strengthens the faithful who are afflicted by illness with the sacrament of anointing, providing them with the strongest means of support.

The celebration of this sacrament consists especially in the laying on of hands by the presbyters of the Church, their offering the prayer of faith, and the anointing of the sick with oil made holy by God's blessing. This rite signifies the grace of the sacrament and confers it.

This sacrament provides the sick person with the grace of the Holy Spirit by which the whole man is brought to health, trust in God is encouraged, and strength is given to resist the temptations of the Evil One and anxiety about death. . . . Thus the sick person is able not only to bear suffering bravely, but also to fight against it. A return to physical health may even follow the reception of this sacrament if it will be beneficial to the sick person's salvation. If necessary, the sacrament also provides the sick person with the forgiveness of sins and the completion of Christian penance" (Introduction, 5-6, Rite of Anointing and Pastoral Care of the Sick).

31. The Apostolic Tradition of Hippolytus, 5, ed. and trans. Burton Scott Easton (Archon Books, 1962), pp. 36-37.

32. Denziger, 91.

33. Smith and Kaluzny, *White Labyrinth*, would be a good starting point for discussion.

34. See Robert L. Kane, Josephine M. Kasteler, Robert M. Gray, eds., *The Health Gap: Medical Services and the Poor* (New York: Springer, 1976); and Charles E. Lewis, Rashi Fein, David Mechanic, *A Right to Health: The Problem of Access to Primary Health Care* (New York: John Wiley, 1976); both works would be helpful for further discussion.

35. E.g., see John R. McIntire, "Samaritan Health Center: An Ecumenical Merger," *Hospital Progress*, 60 (1979), pp. 70-72, 82.

III. The Quest for Justice and Peace

INTRODUCTION

THIS SECTION considers two interrelated themes that figure prominently in both the Catholic and Jewish traditions, flowing as they do from the commonly held vision of the Hebrew prophets. The two are also inherently related, since there can be little hope for a lasting peace without effective justice between peoples, and no hope for justice without the opportunity to build just societal structures that only the full security of peace can provide.

John Pawlikowski reflects on the theological foundations of the relationship between spirituality and the human/divine quest for justice. A fully Catholic spirituality and liturgy, he argues, must foster social engagement in worshipers at the same time as it orients individual and community toward God. Pawlikowski seeks, in short, "an authentically earthly spirituality for our generation."

In his search Pawlikowski adduces testimony from two rather surprising sources (surprising at any rate to many Catholics): Martin Luther and Pharisaic Judaism. The former he sees as "one of the best exponents of late medieval mysticism — namely, that any genuine spiritual experience has to overflow into service of neighbor." The Pharisaic revolution, on the other hand, introduced "the realization of a direct relationship [of the individual] to God, the Father of all people," which came to replace a strict, cultic approach to God. It is the intimate encounter with the covenantal god in both Luther and the Pharisees, Pawlikowski believes, that leads the believer to "burst into action . . . in the service of the people."

Jules Harlow explores the multifaceted concept of *shalom* as utilized in the rabbinic and liturgical traditions of Judaism. *Shalom* means not only "peace," as that word is commonly understood, but wholeness, equity, grace, and prosperity as well. As such, Harlow's essay is one that stitches together all of the various threads of the present volume into a rich tapestry of religious insight. He considers the relationship of peace to prayer and its understanding in the biblical, Messianic tradition.

Whereas Pawlikowski analyzes the development and interpretation of theological principles in the Christian tradition in the light of the church's contemporary dialogue with the Jewish people, Harlow's essay is deeply evocative and textually nuanced. He presents, to use a phrase he himself applies to one of the rabbinic anecdotes he cites, a "case understated with misleading simplicity." Revolving the diamond of Jewish spiritual reflection on peace, Harlow presents facet after facet until a holographic image begins to take on solidity in the reader's mind. In the contrast between the styles of these two essays, the reader will find a paradigm of the unique approaches to spirituality to be discovered in the two traditions thus represented.

Spirituality and
the Quest for Justice

JOHN T. PAWLIKOWSKI

ONE DIMENSION of a theological base for social ethics that has been frequently overlooked, or even deliberately bypassed, has been the relationship between spirituality and the quest for justice. Speaking out of the Catholic tradition, I must add that in fact there has been little reflection on the overall theological foundations of social ethics during the past several centuries. The papal social encyclicals and other recent international Catholic documents such as the II Vatican Declaration on the Church and the Modern World and the 1971 Roman Synod statement on justice have made dents in this gap, but none really provide a comprehensive approach to the question. Pope John Paul II's encyclical *Redemptor Hominis* may come closest to fulfilling the demands for such a comprehensive theological statement. But even these modest attempts at articulating the theological basis for social commitment generally omit any explicit references to the role of spirituality in fostering such engagement.

In addition, the growth of an emphasis on spirituality in the Catholic Church in recent years has frequently led to an unfortunate polarization between its proponents and those men and women who have given their lives to the concrete struggle for a more just and sustainable society nationally and internationally. And if we turn to the Protestant community, where the statement of the theological foundations for social ministry has been far more advanced through the efforts of such theologians as the two Niebuhrs, Walter Muelder, and Gibson Winter, a similar disregard for the role of spirituality in shaping these foundations is likewise readily apparent.

Only very recently have some efforts surfaced to explore the connection between justice and spirituality. In large part these efforts have been spurred by Latin American liberation theology, which, unlike its somewhat earlier cousin — European political theology — has consistently highlighted the crucial nature of the church's liturgical and sacramental traditions in developing a liberated and liberating consciousness within the body of the Catholic community. Another prominent early voice in this regard was the Trappist Thomas Merton, who was in the initial stages of a thorough reevaluation of the issue when his work was cut short by a premature accidental death on an Asian tour.

Within a liberationist context a number of Catholics who have been prominent in various areas of moral responsibility have begun to look at the question. Father Peter Henriot, S.J., attached to the Center of Concern in Washington, is one example. He emphasizes the public dimensions of the spiritual life of Christians in a contribution to a study document on "Social Consciousness and Ignation Spirituality" produced by a Center task force. He writes:

> A consequence of any genuine spiritual renewal, then, is a commitment to the process of action for social justice. Such an action means not merely the performance of good deeds on the level of personal relationships but involves primarily the systematic effort to change unjust social structures. But as important as it may be to see this commitment to act for social justice as being a *consequence* of growth in true spirituality, it is even more important to understand — and to practice — this commitment as being *simultaneous* to the growth process itself. This emphasis upon simultaneity is a more difficult conclusion to demonstrate. It rests upon an

appreciation of the reality of the "public dimension" of personal human existence. Such an appreciation comes with an understanding of social structures and of our own existential relationships with those structures.[1]

At this point I want to make clear my strong commitment to the process of reestablishing links between spirituality and social justice. I think this process is vital if there is to be any hope of retaining a healthy moral tone in this nation and in the world at large. My goal in this presentation is to offer some perspectives on issues I feel need addressing in the quest for an authentically earthly spirituality for our generation. By no means do I offer it as a comprehensive treatment of the subject. That would require a much broader discussion. Also, while I shall be speaking to the issues from a decidedly Catholic perspective, my remarks will always keep an eye open for implications relative to the Christian-Jewish dialogue. Let me emphasize my deep conviction that all of the major religious traditions have much to gain in their own development of a new spirituality that has the pursuit of justice at its core by engagement with other perspectives on the divine/human encounter. Christianity is no exception to this rule. And Christians can profit in particular from an examination of Judaism in this area, given the context that biblical and Pharisaic Judaism provided for the growth of the early Christian community.

Before looking at some contemporary aspects of the question why and how must we link up justice with spiritual growth, it is good to remind ourselves that the question is not an entirely new one. To illustrate this let me turn for a moment to the medieval Christian tradition. My selection of a figure for examination from this period may strike you as a bit strange, for a Catholic and for a Christian-Jewish dialogue setting: Martin Luther. So let me say why the choice. Following the lead of my mentor on Luther, Professor Brian Gerrish of the University of Chicago,[2] I see Luther as one of the best exponents of a major thrust of late medieval mysticism — namely, that any genuine spiritual experience had to overflow into service of neighbor. Because Luther is often appealed to by those who would support a nonservice form of spirituality, in demolishing some myths about the role of works of justice in Luther we open up a whole new understanding of medieval spirituality. I wish to be candid, however, about a hesitancy I have regarding using Luther as a model in the context of the Jewish-Christian dialogue. There is no question in my mind that Luther's writings on the Jewish people deserve a clear and unwavering repudiation. I have indicated my rejection of Luther in this regard in other writings.[3] But despite Luther's reprehensible approach to the Jewish people, he remains a central figure in the history of Christian thought. Hence I feel that given the accessibility of his writings in comparison with some of the other documents representative of medieval mysticism, it is not inappropriate to include him in our reflections on the subject of justice and spirituality as an illustration of a much more extensive approach.

For Luther, the Christian who has been touched by the healing love of Christ in prayer cannot be restrained. He or she breaks out in concrete acts of love toward their neighbors. All one's strength, goods, and even one's very life and reputation must be risked in service of others. To do anything less would be to suffer self-destruction spiritually. This emphasis is especially strong in Luther's volume *The Freedom of a Christian*,[4] where he states without qualification that a person "lives only for others and not for himself" and should act in such a fashion that "he may serve and benefit others in all that he does, considering nothing except the need and the advantage of his neighbor."[5]

The challenge facing interpreters of Luther's writings, once the simplistic notions about his inherent opposition to works have been put aside, concerns the meaning he attached to the notion of righteousness. It is the sense of righteousness in Christ that provides a person with the power to serve others. Luther devotes considerable space to this topic in such essays as *The Freedom of a Christian*, *The Bondage of the Will*, *The Two Kinds of Righteousness*, the *Preface to Romans*, and the *Commentary on Galatians*. His discussion can easily leave the reader rather confused. Only when one recognizes Luther's deep centeredness in the medieval mystical tradition does some clarity began to appear. For Luther this righteousness is nothing short of the full transformation of the human person that brings the fullness of salvation. Brian Gerrish points out that in Luther justification and salvation seem to be virtually synonymous. Once justified the person has faith, which for Luther constitutes the description of the human person after the mystical encounter with God through Christ.[6]

Though Luther's debt to late medieval mysticism is not explicitly acknowledged by him, there are definite indications in several works of its pervasive influence on his doctrine of justification. In one section he describes the effect of the Word on the soul in terms of fire, a favorite mystical category:

> Just as the heated iron glows like fire because of the union of fire with it, so the Word imparts its qualities to the soul.[7]

In another place he speaks of the union of the soul with Christ through faith as a union of bride and bridegroom, another image common to the mystical literature of the period:

> The third incomparable benefit of faith is that it unites the soul with Christ as a bride is united with her bridegroom. By this mystery, as the Apostle teaches, Christ and the soul become one flesh (Eph. 31-32). And if they are one flesh and there is between them a true marriage — indeed, the most perfect of all marriages . . . it follows that everything they have, they hold in common. . . .[8]

In the *Commentary on Galatians* Luther describes God as a consuming fire "in whose sight no flesh is able to stand."[9] Again we are in the presence of the fire imagery of the mystic.

Based on the above evidence I am convinced it is accurate to see Luther as a representative of late medieval mysticism, in which a notion of salvation or justification is rooted in a sense of the all-encompassing transformation of the person resulting from the union of bride and bridegroom, from contact with the consuming fire who is God. This transformation then becomes the source of one's desire to serve one's neighbor. Looked at from another perspective this commitment to social service stands as a barometer of the authenticity of one's salvific transformation. For Luther any attempt at interpreting justification in terms of merit, especially in the crude forms in which it was being preached in his day, or in terms of the ethical and metaphysical categories of Aristotle, is to sacrifice the strictly religious viewpoint of Paul, whose mystical transformation Luther had found to be repeated in his own experience.

Brian Gerrish thus insists that Luther must be seen as a person in revolt against Scholasticism. In so doing he represented the broader movement of late medieval mysticism. Whatever else Luther's critique may represent, and however much I may stand in disagreement with certain dimensions of his theology, his protest against the split between spirituality and commitment to social service introduced by Scholastic theology must be taken with great seriousness today.

At this point it might be well to place Luther's approach to the question of the spirituality/justice link in the context of a study of Judaism. It might be noted at the outset that despite Luther's eventual Hitler-like attack on the Jewish people, he was initially attacked as a "Judaizer" by his opponents. The point of connection that I see here lies in an understanding of the Pharisaic revolution in Judaism, which was directed against the abuses found in the Jewish establishment of the period just prior to and concomitant with the ministry of Jesus. The Pharisees broke the power of the priestly monopoly on salvation whereby the individual Jew had to depend on the priests and the sacrificial system as intermediaries with God. In place of the primacy of priestly, cultic intermediaries, the Pharisees substituted the realization of a direct relationship to God, the Father of all. They spoke of the Father in new terms that are significant for any comparison with Luther. They referred to God as *Makom* ("All Present"), *Shekinah* ("Divine Presence"), and *Ha-Kadosh Barukh Hu* ("Holy One blessed Be He").[10]

All of the above terms point to a notion of a direct divine/human person relationship within Pharisaism that serves as the source of religion and salvation, rather than a strict cultic, intermediary approach. This pharisaic perspective bears strong similarities to the primacy of the mystical contact with God through Christ that is at the heart of Luther's theology. The goal of the Pharisees and of the rabbinic system that developed in their wake was to internalize the halakah system. The abuses of the priestly-sacrificial system, they felt, had reduced the practice of Torah and the offering of sacrifices to an empty ritual. It was only through contact with the presence of the living God of the covenant that the Jew could attain salvation. The emphasis on the covenant was, of course, not unique to the Pharisees. But they did stress the individual in the covenantal relationship in a way that was new to Judaism.[11] It is in response to the experience of the presence of the covenantal God, the Shekinah, that the Jew will burst into action. In this the Jew is similar to the Christian who in Luther's terms has experienced the saving grace of God and will thus bind him or herself to the service of others. The mitzvah for the Pharisaic Jew was a response to a particular communication directed to the individual by God. Holtz says:

> In such an experience, the particular mitzvah which the individual is about to fulfill is not merely a practice transmitted to him by previous generations, but is a command from God here and now.[12]

The mitzvah as a communication from God is viewed in rabbinic thought as a priceless privilege. No one could perform a mitzvah if it were not for the power of God. Max Kadushin puts it this way:

> Having been given that privilege, the individual has a consciousness . . . of belonging to God, of being God's own. At the same time, this entire emotional experience is pervaded through and through with a sense of dedication. The individual dedicates himself to imitate God in acts of Zedakah and Gemilut Hasadim and to abstain from moral Tum'ah. A mystical experience is thus also a source of moral energy, and the more often the experience occurs the greater will be the latent ethical motive power. . . .[13]

The rabbinic emphasis on the necessity of mitzvot as a proper response to the sense of belonging to God is a repetition of the older covenantal attitude that the human person must love because Yahweh first loved him or her and sealed this love in the Mosaic covenant. But in biblical Jewish theology the experience of God's presence took place primarily in the historical events in which God led the people Israel, though the prophets might be somewhat an exception to this norm. The Pharisees, taking their inspiration from the prophets who were the great champions of covenantal morality, made the experience of God the Father's love much more of a reality peculiar to the inner life of each individual person. The mitzvah system they devised to concretize the prophetic summons for a return to covenantal obligation made "communion with God an act that could and should be experienced everywhere and at any time, with or without the Temple, the priest, or the sacrificial altar."[14] For the rabbis a particular mitzvah was always a communication by God here and now.[15]

An interesting rabbinic injunction prescribes the recitation of a berakah (blessing) at the same time a person is performing a mitzvah. The berakah is an expression of gratitude for the privilege of having been given a command here and now by God. Consciousness of the command continues to influence the fulfillment of the mitzvah itself. Otherwise the performance of the deed would lack that experience of personal union with God:

> There is no break in mood from the moment the berakah is begun until the command has been fulfilled; that is to say the recitation of the berakah and the act which follows constitute a unitary experience.[16]

The above observation by Max Kadushin leads into a question that must be probed further in contemporary discussions about the liturgy/justice link. It would be somewhat misleading to understand social service simply as a *consequence* of authentic experience of God. It is that without question. But there is more to the picture. In light of our study of late medieval mysticism and of the rabbinic tradition, we need to appreciate the act of social service as in itself an experience of the presence of God. In part this may be a statement that authentic experience of God must be mediated through human contact, something that the performance of the mitzvah establishes. This realization would recognize the falsity of any approach that would advocate finding God first and only then urge the performance of good deeds for one's neighbor. The relationship is much more intimate. This would, I suggest, have important implications for how we set up styles of prayer for our time.

Overall, then, our study of the Pharisaic tradition and of the tradition of late medieval mysticism examplified in the writings of Martin Luther reveals that they shared in common the desire to make persons aware that salvation is a gift or privilege from God who is the ultimate source of any good action that they perform. Both saw the mystical experience as the way that persons discover this saving power of God. Both revolted against the degradation of religion by a class who had turned it into empty, formal cult. And both were united in the passionate conviction that the experience of God's presence must overflow into service of others.

Based on the above analysis, I am convinced that both Jews and Christians can profit greatly by a study of each other's literature on the subject. We may stumble across commonalities never suspected beforehand. Certainly the writings of, for example, Abraham Heschel, especially (but not exclusively) his notion of *divine pathos* in the prophetic tradition, and of the Jewish mystical tradition will prove of significant value for Christians. One Hasidic mystic phrased the ideal of Jewish mysticism in a simple but effective: "Not the transient upshoot of a straw flame but the well-cooked heart."[17] Rabbi Herbert Weiner would add to this mystic's remark: "Not the sudden and searing flame but the transmutation of that flame into slow warmth which 'tenderized' a human being and made him sensitive to the need of other human beings for bread, pity, and justice — this was the ideal."[18] Weiner, following the great Rabbi Nachman, says that for Judaism the real problem in the mystical experience was not the *r'tzo*, the going out, but the *shuv*, the return. How to transmute the lofty mystical illumination into this-worldly terms was *the problem* that concerned

Jewish mysticism, according to Weiner. Christianity, which has so often experienced a deep polarization between mysticism and the struggle for justice, can learn a great deal from in-depth contact with the Jewish mystical tradition. This is likewise true with regard to the writings of a modern exponent of the mystical tradition, Rav Kook, the first chief rabbi of the modern state of Israel. His writings on the sacramentality of the land have sometimes been compared favorably to the works of the Catholic priest-scientist Father Teilhard de Chardin.

With this brief attempt to illustrate that the problem of the spirituality/justice relationship is not a new one and that resources exist within both our faith traditions for helping us deal with the question in its contemporary expression, let us now turn to the present-day reality. For me, the spirituality/justice problematic has been profoundly influenced by my extensive study of the Nazi Holocaust literature. I have been persuaded by scholars such as the Israeli historian Uriel Tal that the Holocaust represents something more than merely the final, most gruesome sequel in the long, tragic history of Christian anti-Semitism. This is in no way meant to deny the central role that the anti-Semitic tradition exercised in public acceptance of the Nazi "Final Solution." There is little doubt in my mind that classic Christian anti-Semitism provided an indispensable seedbed for Nazism. But the Holocaust also represented the attempt to create a "new person" in an atmosphere in which the new technology combined with bureaucratic efficiency, and the growing collapse of traditional biblical and authoritative religious morality, made possible the virtually unlimited and morally unchallenged use of power to reshape human society and even the human person. Auschwitz truly opened up a new era in human possibility.

Within this perspective the first and, in many ways, the most fundamental reality emerging from an investigation of the Holocaust is how to deal with the human community's new sense of freedom. The Nazis had correctly assessed modern human experience in at least one respect. They rightly understood that profound changes were taking place in human consciousness. Under the impact of the new science and technology, humankind was beginning to undergo a kind of Prometheus Unbound transformation on a mass scale. They now began to become aware of a deeper sense of dignity and autonomy than most of Catholic theology had made room for in the past. Divine punishment, hell, the wrath of God, divine providence—concepts such as these, which had dominated human consciousness since biblical times, were waning in their influence.

This fundamental perceptual change presents a new challenge to all theological interpretation, whether Catholic or Jewish. Although an adequate response will prove difficult for both faith communities, the task will in some ways prove harder for Catholics. Jews can summon some traditional themes from their religious literature, such as the notion of salvation as an incomplete process still taking place within the confines of history, of the human person as cocreator of the universe, and of the sense of humanity's independence from God most dramatically conveyed in the story of Jacob's "wrestling with God." These notions have largely disappeared from the average Catholic's understanding of the divine/human person encounter.

The task facing Catholic theology will be to find a way to affirm the new sense of human freedom being born in our time, while suggesting constructive outlets for its expression. It cannot simply ignore or deny the existence of this new sense of freedom, an approach that still, unfortunately, obtains in sectors of Catholicism. A significant alteration in our understanding of the divine/human person relationship is called for in the light of Auschwitz.

Yet the new sense of human liberation to which the Holocaust formed a destructive response cannot be endorsed naively by contemporary Catholic theology. Post-Holocaust Catholic theology needs to begin to articulate an understanding of God and religion that will prevent the newly discovered creative powers of the human person from being transformed into the destructive force we have seen exposed in all its ugliness in the Holocaust. It must begin grappling with the pervasive condition of twentieth-century humanity, a period in which, as the philosopher Hans

Jonas has poignantly described, "we shiver in the nakedness of a nihilism in which near omnipotence is paired with near emptiness, greatest capacity with knowing least what for."[19]

The post-Auschwitz divine/human person relationship will need to be one in which there is a clear recognition of God's utter and inescapable dependence upon the human community in the process of salvation. The God whom we used to invoke through our prayers to intervene and correct the ills of the world died in the ashes of the Holocaust. God will not intervene to stop perversions of authentic human freedom. Auschwitz has taught us that God will not, perhaps even cannot, effect the full redemption of that part of his being that he has graciously shared with humankind unless human beings assume their appointed role of cocreators.

But for the human community to assume this cocreatorship role without falling into the practice of destructiveness that dominated Nazism there is need for present-day theology to articulate a notion of transcendence that can counterbalance this potential for such destructiveness. Any theology that fails to grapple seriously with this phenomenon of destructiveness — the underside of human freedom — will ultimately fall by the wayside. A theology will have to be built that can truly guide this growing sense of human freedom and power.

Theology alone will not be able, however, to open up this newly required sense of transcendence. And this is where the connection between liturgy/spirituality and social commitment becomes crucial. This new sense of transcendence will have to emerge from experiments in religious experience; it will require a new appreciation of religious symbolism. Persons once more will need to experience contact with a personal power beyond themselves, a power that heals the destructive tendencies still lurking within humanity. The newly liberated person, to be able to work consistently toward the creation of a just and humane society, must begin to sense that there exists a judgment upon human endeavor that goes beyond mere human judgment. The old sense of judgment rooted in a notion of divine punishment will no longer work. The modern experience of the human community is that the worst atrocities can be perpetrated with apparent impunity. The only norm that can finally curb such atrocities is one rooted in an experience of love and unity beyond the narrow dimensions of this earth, along with the concomitant realization that actions such as those that shaped the Holocaust ultimately block the attainment of such love and unity. This understanding must become a deeply-felt perception of the human community and not merely a theological idea. And such a perception, I am increasingly persuaded, will arise only from immersion in spirituality and liturgy.

In order to adequately deal with the new creative power inherent in the freedom that has come to the human community in our day, persons will need to develop a basic moral sensitivity as a prelude to moral reasoning. This sensitivity will involve the growth of a sense of such realities as sin, freedom, dependence, solidarity, vulnerability, and oppression. Liturgy and spirituality are essential to such growth in the consciousness of individuals and of the larger community of humankind.

Let me state very clearly the full implications of my thought. I am saying that in my perspective, based on an analysis of such events as the Holocaust, reason by itself is judged incapable of providing the kind of moral sensitivity required to meet the ethical demands of our day. Without question, reason has a role. But it is one that follows upon moral sensitivity. Spiritual experience left unattended by reason can easily fall into the trap of moral fanaticism. As I see it this is a challenging conclusion for both Jewish and Catholic ethics that have deeply depended upon reason as a source of moral behavior. Priorities here must be rethought. I think a Holocaust commentator such as Irving Greenberg is perfectly right when he argues that Auschwitz has undercut the validity of any ethic based solely on the possibilities of human reason.[20] This conclusion is also very much in line with what a Catholic ethician such as Daniel Maguire has been saying in his recent writings.[21] Beyond the development of any "cause liturgies" emphasizing hunger, the environment, and so forth, the more basic ethical dimensions of liturgy and spirituality need to be recognized and promoted — their role in the growth of fundamental moral perceptions without which most individuals will lack the courage or the conviction to stand up for justice and peace in our time.

This liturgy/spirituality approach to the development of moral sensitivity on a personal and communal level must be anchored, from the Catholic perspective, in a consciousness-oriented Christology focused on the notion of the incarnation. I cannot lay out the dimensions of this Christological understanding in any comprehensive manner in this presentation. I have recently completed a book on the subject. A skeletal outline of my position is available in several of my published articles.[22] The best I can do here is offer a thumbnail sketch.

In the incarnation, as I understand it, the growing sense of human uniqueness and dignity was initially expressed in the Genesis theology of the human person as God's cocreator. It was further developed in the Pharisaic emphasis on the worth and status of each individual person. Human persons now realized that they shared in the very life and existence of God. The human person was still creature; there remained a profound gulf between humanity in human persons and humanity in the Godhead. But it was clear that a direct link also existed; the two humanities could touch. The human struggle for self-identity vis-à-vis the Creator-God had come to an end in principle, though its full realization still lay ahead. In this sense we can truly say that Christ brought and continues to bring humankind salvation in its root sense: wholeness. With a proper understanding of the meaning of the Christ event, men and women can be healed, they can finally overcome the primal sin of pride — the desire to supplant the Creator in power and status — because they have seen in the cross the self-imposed limitations of the Father. We now see that our destiny is to live forever in our uniqueness and individuality. God will not finally try to absorb us totally back into his being. In fact it has become apparent that God must allow men and women this degree of eternal distinctiveness in order to reach full maturity himself, to become finally and fully God.

I might add at this point that, although not denying some profound differences, there do exist similarities between this incarnational Christological approach and the Pharisaic movement in Judaism. The latter undertook a significant internalization of Jewish religious understanding that, I would argue, had a definite impact on Christological development in early Christianity. This internalization process in Pharisaic Judaism and its connection with Christian Christological formulation is detailed by the Jewish historian Ellis Rivkin in his many writings on the subject.[23]

Another point that is relevant to our concern with the link between spirituality/liturgy and justice is the fact that the incarnational Christology briefly described above has its origins in a liturgical setting. This conclusion seems confirmed by some of the research of Father Raymond Brown into the subject.[24] This serves to underscore my belief that for Christians the primary Christological underpinning for social commitment must come not from systematic theology but from the liturgical/spiritual experience.

I must issue a cautionary note regarding my Christological approach. Too often incarnational Christology has led to antisocial attitudes on the part of Christians. This is obviously quite removed from what I am advocating. The incarnational Christology that I propose must ultimately be understood as the revelation to the human family that its humanity can be made whole because of the human capacity to be touched in the deepest realms of consciousness by the humanity of God and its saving power. This provides history with a vital new significance. For what men and women are doing in and through the historical process is trying to establish political and social structures that will enhance the consciousness of persons and bring about the possibility of their ultimate communion, while preserving some degree of individuality and uniqueness. Social and political structures are a reflection of human consciousness; they also aid or detract from the growth of human consciousness. This is the insight captured by Teilhard de Chardin when he wrote:

> Note this well: I attribute no definite and absolute value to the various constructions of man. I believe they will disappear, recast in a new whole that we cannot yet conceive. At

the same time I admit that they have an essential provisional role — that they are necessary, inevitable phases through which we (we or the race) must pass in the course of our metamorphosis. What I love in them is not their particular form, but their function, which is to build up, in some mysterious way, first something divinizable — and then, through the grace of Christ alighting on our effort, something divine.[25]

There are two key points to be grasped. First, there exists an intimate link between history and human consciousness. Here Father Peter Henriot's remarks about the prayer/social-structure connections quoted at the beginning of this paper are very pertinent. One cannot really understand fully the intimate link between prayer/liturgy and social commitment without a profound apreciation of the relationship between consciousness and social structures. Secondly, salvation, in the final analysis, involves the ability to establish communion with God and neighbor through the healing that results from greater contact between human consciousness and the humanity of God as a consequence of the destruction of dehumanizing socio-political structures. Socio-political structures that establish patterns of oppression and injustice thus block the realization of that depth of human consciousness where salvation and the final kingdom are ultimately to be located.

To round off my articulation of the Christological basis for the spirituality/social-commitment link, I should like to offer a working definition of social justice. As I see it, justice in a sociopolitical context can be described as "the process of changing the relationships among persons from those of dominance and oppression to those of respect, equality, and possible intercommunion. Justice will be accomplished through the creation of new cultural, political, and economic patterns that enhance human dignity, communal consciousness, and interpersonal communication, facilitate contemplation, and ensure the survival of the physical universe for future generations on the path toward the ultimate reconciliation of human and divine consciousness." This definition needs elaboration on many points, something I do not have the time to do here. Suffice it to say that I see the experience of the Christ who is the humanity of God within the prayer/liturgical experience as central to the advancement of this process of justice. But it is likewise important to note that because I view enhanced contemplation as one of the principal results of the achievement of greater social justice, the relationship between spirituality and justice is not a one-way street. Because, in my understanding, ultimate salvation occurs in the realm of consciousness, the just society must create patterns of living that will facilitate the opportunity for inner self-development — always, however, within a firm commitment to community. This is the reason incidentally why personal prayer is insufficient by itself in this context. The liturgical dimension that highlights community is indispensable. The opportunity to develop the inner-consciousness side of the human person must never be allowed to degenerate into excessive individualism and its consequent antisocietal form of human behavior.

An additional issue that can be raised regarding the spirituality/society-justice link is the potential value of prayer/liturgy for sustaining the personal commitment of those engaged in social ministry. It is clear from experience that any attempt at the creation of a just society not undergirded by an abiding spirituality will quickly burn itself out. An authentic and healing experience of God's presence made possible through participation in the Eucharist and other forms of prayer is necessary to maintain the commitment to justice in the face of the inevitable failure, frustration, and hostility that such a commitment entails for the life of the Christian steward. The prayer experience is needed to keep up a high level of moral energy. It is also necessary to prevent almost certain hostility and failure from leading committed Christians to withdraw Qumran-style from the world or become so embittered that an anarchist temptation takes root within them.

My final point is a rather sensitive one in the dialogue. If we are to accept in principle the profound link between spirituality and social justice, then I feel the Jewish community will have to rethink its position of opposition to dialogical prayer/liturgy possibilities expressed in such statements as the official response of the International Jewish Liaison Committee to the 1975 Vatican Guidelines on Catholic-Jewish Relations, which stressed the value of joint prayer. I realize how delicate an issue this is and I can appreciate Jewish hesitation. But a staunch and definite *No* seems to run counter to the basic thrust of the new under-standing of the spirituality/social-justice relationship that is emerging in both the Jewish and Christian communities.[26] I should hope that organized Jewry might find it possible to reexamine its stand on this question. I do not think it sufficient for us merely to talk about the issue; I am convinced that in addition we must find at least occasional moments when we can share the healing/expanding experience of liturgy and prayer together, to bolster our common commitment to the cause of justice.

NOTES

1. "The Public Dimension of the Spiritual Life of the Christian: The Problem of 'Simultaneity,' " *Soundings*, 1974, p. 13.

2. See *Grace and Reason* (Oxford: Clarendon Press, 1962).

3. See "Martin Luther and Judaism: Paths Towards Theological Reconciliation," *Journal of the American Academy of Religion*, 43 (Dec. 1975), pp. 681-93.

4. See John Dillenberger, *Martin Luther: Selections from His Writings* (New York: Anchor Books, 1961).

5. Ibid., p. 73.

6. Gerrish, *Grace*, pp. 125-26, 135-36.

7. Dillenberger, *Martin Luther*, p. 58.

8. Ibid., p. 60.

9. Ibid., p. 142.

10. On the pharisaic movement, see Ellis Rivkin, "The Internal City," *Journal for the Scientific Study of Religion*, 5 (Spring 1966), pp. 232-34; idem, "The Pharisaic Background of Christianity," in *Root and Branch: The Jewish-Christian Dialogue*, Michael Zeik and Martin Siegel, eds. (Williston Park, N.Y.: Roth, 1973); idem, *The Hidden Revolution* (Nashville: Abingdon, 1978); Jacob Neusner, *From Politics to Piety: The Emergence of Pharisaic Judaism* (Englewood Cliffs, N.J.: Prentice-Hall, 1973); John T. Pawlikowski, "On Renewing the Revolution of the Pharisees," *Cross Currents*, 20 (Fall 1970), pp. 415-34; idem, *Sinai and Calvary: The Meeting of Two Peoples* (Beverly Hills, Cal.: Benziger, 1976).

11. See Rivkin, "Internal City," pp. 232-34.

12. J. Holtz, "Kiddush Hashem and Hillul Hashem," *Judaism*, 10 (1961), pp. 360 ff.

13. *Worship and Ethics: A Study in Rabbinic Judaism* (Evanston, Ill.: Northwestern University Press, 1964), pp. 232-33.

14. Stuart E. Rosenberg, "Contemporary Renewal and the Jewish Experience," paper delivered at the 1968 International Conference of Christians and Jews, York University, Toronto, September 1968, p. 3.

15. Kadushin, *Worship*, p. 225.

16. Ibid., p. 234.

17. See Herbert Weiner, *9 1/2 Mystics: The Kabbala Today* (New York: Holt, Rinehart and Winston, 1969), pp. 304-5.

18. Ibid., p. 305.

19. See *Philosophical Essays* (Boston: Beacon, 1974), p. 124.

20. See "Cloud of Smoke, Pillar of Fire: Judaism, Christianity and Modernity after the Holocaust," in Eva Fleischner, ed., *Auschwitz: Beginning of a New Era?* (New York: Ktav, 1977), p. 17.

21. See *The Moral Choice* (Garden City, N.Y.: Doubleday, 1978).

22. See my *Christ in the Light of the Jewish-Christian Dialogue* (Paulist, 1982) and my essays "Christ and the Jewish-Christian Dialogue," *Chicago Studies*, 16 (Fall 1977), pp. 367-90, and "The Historicizing of the Eschatological; The Spiritualizing of the Eschatological: Some Reflections," in Alan T. Davis, ed., *Antisemitism and the Foundations of Christianity* (New York: Paulist Press, 1979), pp. 151-66.

23. See his *A Hidden Revolution* and "The Pharisaic Background of Christianity."

24. See "Does the New Testament Call Jesus God?," *Theological Studies*, (Dec. 1965).

25. Letter, Dec. 12, 1919.

26. See the special issue of the *Journal of Religious Ethics* devoted to this topic: vol. 7, no. 2 (Fall 1979).

Peace in Traditional
Jewish Expression

JULES HARLOW

ONE OF THE MOST COMMONLY USED WORDS in Hebrew is shalom, familiar to non-Jews as well as to Jews. You do not have to be Jewish or a Hebrew scholar to know that shalom means peace. It is also a greeting, and used in modern Hebrew to say goodbye as well as hello. On the Sabbath, the greeting is: *Shabbat Shalom.*

It could be more than a bit startling, then, to be confronted with a prohibition forbidding the use of the word "shalom" in any context. Yet precisely that is contained in what must appear to some as a bewildering mass of details constituting Jewish religious practice. The Talmud states that it is forbidden to use the word "shalom" in the bathhouse,[1] just as other sources proscribe its use in what we now refer to as the bathroom. Why? Because shalom, peace, is the name of God, which is not to be bandied about in an unclean place.

In the Talmud this association is presented as having begun with Gideon, who built an altar that he called "The Lord is peace" (Judg. 6:24). Whatever the origin, this identification of God with peace clearly declares that peace is precious, assigning it the highest value possible and attempting to raise it out of what could be a routine fate: being treated as another cliché, merely a platitude. Peace is holy.

In order to avoid possible confusion, it might be useful at this point to emphasize that "peace" is not the only connotation or specific meaning of the Hebrew word "shalom." In biblical Hebrew, shalom can mean complete or loyal. Shalom also means health, well-being, prosperity, safety, integrity, equity, grace, friendship, and alliance.[2]

In postbiblical literature too, as stated by George Foote Moore:

> [Shalom] has a wider meaning than the English "peace." For the individual it is welfare of every kind, sound health, prosperity, security, contentment and the like. In the relations of men to their fellows it is the harmony without which the welfare of the individual or the community is impossible; aggression, enmity and strife are destructive of welfare, as external and internal peace, in our sense, is its fundamental condition.[3]

We shall be considering shalom as peace. Peace is precious, it is holy, of highest value. In the worldview of the ancient rabbis, the world would not be possible without it. In the second century, "Rabban Shimon ben Gamaliel said that the world is sustained by three things: by truth, by justice and by peace."[4] Another rabbinic source declares the three to be synonymous, for when justice is carried out, truth is vindicated and peace is effected.[5]

For the ancient rabbis, peace is equal to all of creation.[6] Without peace, there is nothing.[7] Why did God begin humanity by creating a single individual rather than three or ten or more human beings? The rabbis taught that a single human being was created for the sake of peace among creatures. If all human beings have a common ancestor in Adam, no one can claim to anyone else "My father is greater than your father."[8] A single common ancestor hampers competitive struggles between families. And should you question this by telling me to open my eyes to look at reality, which abounds with contentiousness, I would respond in the spirit of the talmudic discussion on the topic: You think that it is bad now? Think how bad it would have been if there were *several* ancestors equal in origin, not just the single Adam![9]

In the biblical account of creation, each day is crowned with the declaration that "God saw how good this was," with one exception: the second day. On the second day God separated the water that was below the expanse from the water that was above it. A day that introduced *division* to the world cannot be called good. That this is so even though this particular division was for the benefit of creation, highlights the disastrous consequences of a division introduced without such good intentions or salutary benefits.[10] The very concept of division stands in the way of peace.

To paraphrase Job (25:1), God makes peace on high, God ordains the order of the universe. The rabbis saw this order, this peaceful coexistence, in the upper spheres, reflected in the fact that the dark side of the moon never faces the sun. When the moon begins to wane, the process is started at the portion farthest from the sun, they state. These orderings were made to insure that the moon will not be disgraced or embarrassed, making possible the peaceful, harmonious coexistence of two unequal heavenly bodies — an example of the details arranged by God for the sake of peace on high.[11]

God's ways in arranging for order in the universe are to be taken as a model for human behavior on earth. The powerful have obligations that might not even occur to those of lesser position. Harmony is a goal, an ideal that is realizable and well worth the effort required. God built peace and harmony into the very act of creation, for he was conscious of possible conflicts. His creation reflects a balance, a conscious blending, of the upper and the lower spheres, the ethereal and the mundane. Thus we are taught that on the first day he created from both spheres — heaven and earth. The firmament of the second day and the lights of the fourth day represent the higher spheres, just as the waters of the third day and the swarming creatures of the fifth day represent the lower spheres. Thus far there is a balance, which might possibly be upset on the sixth day, the day of human creation. Therefore the human being was created from both spheres, with "dust of the earth" from the lower sphere and with "the breath of life" from the higher sphere.[12]

Harmony in human behavior follows the divine model. The people Israel were deemed worthy of the gift of revelation only when they exhibited their unity. This important lesson is derived stylistically from grammatical clues in the biblical narrative. A rabbinic homily begins with a verse from the Book of Numbers (33:5) stating that the Israelites set out from Raamses and encamped at Succoth. In this verse and in subsequent verses describing their travels, plural Hebrew verbs are used for "set out" and "encamped" (*va-ya-hanu*), reflecting the reality that their life as a community during these journeys was characterized by disputes, a lack of unity. When they approached Mount Sinai, however, they behaved as one encampment, united, a reality reflected in the singular verb form describing the Israelite community in the wilderness of Sinai. "Israel encamped (*va-yihan*) there in front of the mountain" (Exod. 19:2). They were living in harmony, at peace with one another. The homily concludes: "Said the Holy One, 'This is the appropriate time for giving the Torah to My children.' "[13]

The spirit of the members of a community and the way that its members live together reflects the quality of their life and the values they embrace. That spirit can also affect the prayer of the community, for prayer is not a magic formula; the recitation of the words of prayer does not guarantee a result in the absence of other factors. Thus we are told that the prayers of a congregation will go unnoticed if there is no peace among its members. In an interpretation of a verse from Jeremiah (33:6) we are taught that when prayer contains the spirit of peace it is truth, but if it does not contain the spirit of peace it is untruth.[14]

At the end of the second century Rabbi Shimon ben Halafta taught that all blessings are useless if unaccompanied by peace. Peace is the vessel most appropriate for containing blessing. "Blessing" here refers not only to that which is good but to blessing as prayer, with Rabbi Shimon citing the fact that the final benediction in the series of benedictions at the center of Jewish prayer has peace as its focus.[15] Why is the blessing of peace the final blessing of these benedictions (which are also known collectively as the Silent Prayer, or Standing Prayer, or ʿAmidah)?

At the end of each service of sacrificial worship in the ancient Temple, the priests would bless the people. This is traced to Leviticus (9:22) where we read that following the sacrificial service Aaron (the high priest) lifted his hands toward the people and blessed them. In fourteenth-century Spain, a liturgical commentator (Abudarham) explained that since after the destruction of the Temple the rabbis ordained that words of prayer be offered in place of the daily sacrifices, the priestly blessings should conclude the central prayer, as indeed it concluded the sacrificial service.[16]

What is the content of that blessing? It is found in the Book of Numbers: "The Lord spoke to Moses, saying, Speak to Aaron and his sons. 'Thus shall you bless the people Israel: May the Lord bless you and keep you. May the Lord show you favor and be gracious to you. May the Lord show you kindness and grant you peace' "(Num. 6:22-26).

During the repetition by the cantor of the series of benedictions known as the ʿAmidah, the formalized benediction is included:

> Grant peace, goodness, blessing, grace, love and mercy to us and to all the people Israel. Bless us, our Father, one and all, with Your light, for by that light did You grant us Torah and life, love and tenderness, justice, blessing, mercy and peace. May it please You to bless Your people Israel at every season and at all times with Your peace. Praised are you, Lord who blesses His people Israel with peace.

The priestly benediction (from Num. 6) is one of the three prayers singled out in a rabbinic homily declaring that peace is great, for all blessings and consolations that the Holy One brings to the people Israel are sealed with peace.[17] The prayers specified are:

(1) The recitation of "Hear, O Israel" (Deut. 6:4 plus additional biblical passages) and its accompanying benedictions, which end, in the evening service for Sabbath and holidays, with words praising God "who spreads a shelter of peace over us, over all His people Israel and over Jerusalem." (The Hebrew word

for peace is incorporated into the very name of the holy city.)

(2) The conclusion of a meditation following the Amidah — a conclusion consisting of words taken from part of a verse from Job (25:1), stating and beseeching, "He who makes peace for His universe will make peace for us and for all the people Israel."

(3) The priestly benediction (Num. 6) cited above, concluding with the words, "May the Lord show you kindness and grant you peace." This benediction is not recited by the individual, but by the cantor during the repetition of the ʿAmidah, when it is followed by the formalized benediction of peace.

To begin an appreciation of how these texts are understood in Jewish tradition, we shall review some statements of ancient rabbis and modern liturgical commentators, approaching the three selections in reverse order.

The last words of the priestly benediction are taken to imply something about our relationships with others, not only about what we might expect from God. A compilation from seventeenth- to eighteenth-century Eastern Europe comments on the final words of this blessing — "and grant you peace" — "Peace when you approach and peace when you take your leave, peace with everyone."[18] Rabbi Jacob Zvi Mecklenberg of nineteenth-century Germany, commenting on the same words, identifies that peace as "the peace of Torah . . . inner peace, peace of the spirit, peace free of the confusion and conflict of natural desires which are at war with the ways of Torah and its commandments."[19]

The meditation after the benedictions of the ʿAmidah concludes with "He who makes peace for His universe will make peace for us and for all the people Israel." These words also conclude the doxology known as the Kaddish in its full form. As noted above, some of these words are taken from a verse in Job (25:1) that reads, "Dominion and fear are with God who makes peace in His high heavens." The last half of the verse is taken to mean that God makes an effort to arrange for peaceful coexistence in the upper spheres, also noted above. Inasmuch as God has accomplished this on high, we pray that he will do the same for mortals below, on earth.

Part of God's uniqueness is reflected in his ability to make peace between opposites, making it possible for fire and water to abide together, in an ancient rabbinic example. God used both fire and water in creating the firmament known as heaven (*shamayim* in Hebrew, resounding with *esh*, fire, and *mayim*, water).[20] This union of opposites, essential to peace, is also crucial to the peaceful coexistence of two important angels—Michael, who consists of snow, and Gabriel, who consists of fire. They serve together without harming one another. Bar Kappara, of third-century Palestine, draws a lesson from this: heavenly beings are free of jealousy and hatred and competition, yet they require the reality of peace for coexistence; all the more so is peace required for earthly beings, who consist of competition and hatred and jealousy.[21]

"Grant peace, goodness, and blessing. . . . " These words begin the benediction of peace following the Priestly Benediction. Rabbi Mecklenberg specifies that this particular order is required in the nature of things:

> [For] if there is no peace among us there is no place for goodness and blessing to rest. Thus our Sages have taught in the Mishnah that the Holy One found peace to be the only vessel capable of holding blessing for the people Israel. And we see in the natural order of things that a vessel must first be in perfect order before placing its appropriate contents within it.[22]

Since peace is the only appropriate vessel for blessing, notes Rabbi Johathan Eybeschutz of eighteenth-century Prague, "pray that there be no dissension among the people Israel, that they be free of jealousy and hatred and strife . . . . Let them all be loving, united . . . as one . . . to fulfill the Torah's injunction to love your neighbor as yourself," for this is the essence of prayer. Furthermore, he writes, we should pray to be freed of the attribute of anger, that we might be humble before all, which is necessary to attain the level of peace, for peace and anger cannot abide together.[23]

Rabbi Elijah, the Gaon of eighteenth-century Vilna, is quoted by Rabbi Mecklenberg in the following century as declaring that whosoever is aroused with anger is comparable to an idolater, the ultimate desecration. Why such a drastic comparison? To emphasize the special importance of human relationships in the Jewish scheme of things, for they are the essence of Torah. "We ask for God's blessings of love and compassion in our own lives. So should we invoke God's help, that we may treat others with love and compassion, treating them justly, to bring blessing in the midst of life on earth and to love the peace that resides in our midst."[24]

Jewish tradition demands a close reading of sacred texts, both to understand their literal meaning and to understand their unstated implications, the values conveyed by those texts. Thus Rabbi Isaac Elijah Landau, of nineteenth-century Vilna, considers the words, "Grant peace . . . to us and to all the people Israel," and asks a question based upon language and usage. What if an individual is praying alone, not as part of a congregation? Would it not be correct for him or her to say, "Grant peace . . . to *me* " rather than "to *us*"? That would make sense however, only if we ignored the essential teaching that peace demands the harmonization of opposites. The individual must seek peace by intending to have no conflict, whether with God on high or with other creatures on earth. Peace is not strengthened by individuals acting alone, but through the interaction of at least two opposites. Therefore, an individual in prayer should indeed pray, "Grant peace to *us*," implying that peace be granted "to me together with those who oppose me."[25]

Peace between one human being and another is *not* the concern of the prayer that concludes the recital of "Hear O Israel" and its accompanying benedictions, in the view of Rabbi Mecklenberg.[26] "Spread over us the shelter of Your peace" refers to peace between man and God, the peace of Torah, which demands that physical desires be subjugated to the Torah and its commandments. One who has attained the balance, who fulfills the commandments out of love and who rejoices in the service of God, with inner peace, still requires God's help: various temptations assault that inner peace and it is sometimes difficult to withstand the forces of wickedness and desire that becloud the light of Torah in the human soul. Therefore we pray for God's protection, that we may be sheltered by his peace.

The early morning service contains the following rabbinic passage, which again highlights the importance of peace:

> These are the commandments which yield immediate fruit in this world and which will continue to yield fruit in the world to come: Honoring parents, doing deeds of lovingkindness, attending the house of study punctually, morning and evening, providing hospitality, visiting the sick, helping the needy bride, attending the dead, devotion in prayer and *making peace between one person and another* [italics added; some texts continue: "And between husband and wife"]. And the study of Torah is basic to them all.

Rabbi Simeon ben Yohai of the second century stated that all blessings are contained in peace, citing a verse from the Book of Psalms (29:11) that appears often in Jewish liturgy: "may the Lord grant strength to His people, may the Lord bless His people with peace."[27]

The wedding service includes a blessing praising God "who created joy and gladness, bride and groom, mirth, song, delight and rejoicing, love and harmony, peace and companionship." This passage is reminiscent of the blessing recited at the changing of the watch in the ancient Temple in Jerusalem. The outgoing watch would say to those beginning their service: "May He who causes His name to dwell in this House cause love and harmony, peace and companionship to dwell among you."[28]

The very construction of the ancient Temple reflects traditional Jewish attitudes about peace. David, traditionally the singer of psalms and the king of Israel, was not allowed to build the Temple. Why not?

> David said to Solomon: "My son, I had intended to build a house honoring the name of the Lord my God. But the word of the Lord came to me, saying, 'You have shed much blood and have waged great wars. For this reason you shall not build a house honoring My name. But you shall have a son who

shall be a man of peace. I will give him peace from all of his enemies on every side; Solomon shall be his name and I will grant peace and quiet to Israel in his days. He shall build a house in honor of My name.' "[29]

Religious institutions must reflect their stated high principles and commitment to holiness even in technical details of structure. The essential commitment to peace must thus be reflected in the building of the altar. This tradition begins in the Torah. "You shall build an altar of stones to the Lord your God. Do not wield an iron tool over them" (Deut. 27:5). "And if you make for Me an altar of stones, do not build it of hewn stones; for by wielding a tool upon them you have profaned them" (Exod. 20:22). Why is it forbidden to use iron in building an altar? Because, we are taught, iron is used in forging a sword, which is the symbol of curse, whereas the altar is the symbol of atonement, indeed it effects ritual atonement.

The Book of Deuteronomy instructs, "You must build the altar of the Lord your God of unhewn stones ('*avanim shleimot*)." This last word is related to shalom. The unhewn stones must embody shalom — completion, wholeness, perfection — constitutive elements of peace. A rabbinic teaching on this verse states:

Stones cannot hear, speak, eat or drink. Yet because they make peace between the people Israel and their Father in Heaven, the Torah ordains that they must be whole, perfect. How much more should this be true for those people who are suffused with Torah; they too must be perfect, whole before the Holy One, for they too can bring atonement to the world.[30]

This is the challenge of religious leadership if it is to be wholesome, a force for peace.

A challenge to political and religious institutions, demanding that they not be self-serving, is posed by the twentieth-century Rabbi Marcus Wald's interpretation of a talmudic passage: "The son of David (i.e., the Messiah) will come only when the governments change their way and become heretics"[31] — which is to say, when they stop waging wars in the name of religion.

Peace is not passive. Peace is a quest. In the words of the

Psalmist (34:15), "Turn from evil and do good, seek peace and pursue it." In the rabbinic view too, peace must be pursued if it is to be maintained. The Torah does not demand that the commandments be pursued. When certain situations present themselves, one is obliged to respond appropriately. For example, "When you encounter your enemy's ox or donkey wandering, you must take it back to him" (Exod. 23:4). "When you see the donkey of your enemy lying under its burden . . . you must raise it with him" (Exod. 23:5). Peace, however, you must *seek* wherever you are, and peace you must *pursue* everywhere.

This attitude is exemplified in the behavior of Moses, who was told that Sihon the Amorite was "given into his power." Moses was directed to begin the occupation, to engage Sihon in battle (Deut. 2:24). Yet Moses and the people pursued peace, for we read two verses later (Deut. 2:26) that Moses sent messengers from the wilderness of Kedemot to Sihon with an offering of peace, pursuing peace and setting an example for all time.[32]

"Great is peace," said Rabbi Yossi Ha-gallili at the beginning of the second century, "for even in time of war, attempts at peace must precede all else, as it is written, 'When you approach a city to attack it, you must offer it terms of peace' " (Deut. 20:10).[33]

Isaiah's extraordinary vision of peace among nations has been called "the last word" on the subject. Too often it has not been considered as the first world.

> In time to come the mount of the Lord's Temple shall stand
> firm above the mountains, towering above the hills,
> and all nations shall turn their attention to it.
> Many nations shall go there, saying:
> "Come, let us journey to the mount of the Lord,
> to the Temple of the God of Jacob,
> that He may teach us His way, that we may walk in His
>   paths."
> For instruction shall be coming from Zion,
> the word of the Lord from Jerusalem.
> He will decide the disputes between nations,
> and arbitrate for the multitude of peoples.
> They shall beat their swords into plowshares,

and their spears into pruning hooks.
Nation shall not lift up sword against nation,
nor shall they experience war any more [Isa. 2:1-4].

A rabbinic comment based on this passage states that when the
Messiah comes, weapons will not be needed. Weapons then will
be as superfluous as a candle at high noon.[34]

Consider the great power of peace, begins another rabbinic
homily. Creatures of flesh and blood never forget any harm that
is done to their friends. This is not true of the Holy One. The
people Israel while in Egypt were subjugated harshly through
mud and bricks. Yet after all the evils that the Egyptians inflicted
upon the people Israel, scripture shows mercy for the Egyptians,
commanding, "You shall not abhor an Egyptian, for you were
a stranger in his land" (Deut. 23:8). Rather should you pursue
peace, as it is written, "Seek peace and pursue it."[35]

Rabbinic ancedotes reveal worlds of meaning, sustaining us
with both charm and instruction, transforming superficial, trivial
incidents, because all statements of the rabbis were informed by
a vision of the holy. It is related that a certain Rav Beroka,
visiting a marketplace, came across Elijah the prophet and seized
the opportunity to ask Elijah: "Is there anyone in this marketplace who deserves life in the world to come?" Elijah answered,
"No." Just then two men entered the marketplace and Elijah
pointed them out. "Those two are deserving of life in the world
to come." Rav Beroka approached them. "Tell me about
yourselves." They responded, "We are happy men who try to
make sad people happy. And whenever we see two people in
the midst of an argument we take the trouble to make peace between them."[36]

The case is understated with unintentionally misleading
simplicity. Peacemaking is not easy, but that is the whole point
about making peace. The two men in the marketplace "take the
trouble" to make peace. Rabbi Naham of Bratslav, living in the
Ukraine of the eighteenth and nineteenth centuries, put it quite
well:

The main function of peace is joining two opposites. Do not
be upset when you encounter someone who maintains an

opinion completely contrary to yours, do not assume that it is impossible to maintain a peaceful relationship with him. When you see two people who are absolute opposites, do not say that it is impossible to make peace between them. On the contrary, this is the main function of peace: You must try to make peace between two opposites.[37]

Jonah Gerondi, a rabbi of thirteenth-century Spain, urged that "Jews must pick out select men who will impose peace, who will be able to run after people and enforce peace. These select men should be capable of mollifying and conciliating others, capable of imposing peace."[38]

Aaron is the model of peace for the ancient rabbis, even though there is no specific biblical verse that identifies him as such. "Be disciples of Aaron, loving peace and pursuing peace."[39] A later source, expanding upon this statement, applies a verse from Malachi (2:6) to Aaron: "The Torah of truth (true instruction) was on his tongue, and no word of injustice ever fell from his lips; he walked in peace and in righteousness with Me and he turned many back from sin." The last words of this verse are exemplified in the life of Aaron, the teaching continues. What would an Aaron do as a pursuer of peace? He would go to great lengths, seeking out persons who had fallen into arguments, going first to one and then to the other, telling each how badly the other was feeling, persisting with each of them until the two of them were able to come together in peace.[40]

Peace in a household is seen as essential to the peace of the entire community, just as jealousy and contention within a household have a profoundly negative impact upon the entire community.[41] The extremes to which one must go to maintain family peace are illustrated in a story related about Aaron and told in an expanded way about Rabbi Meir of second-century Palestine. It seems that a certain lady attended his lectures, which she found quite fascinating for she returned to her own home rather late. Upon learning the reason for her tardiness, her husband forbade her to enter their home again without spitting in the eye of Rabbi Meir. After two weeks of living away from home, she went with her neighbors to see Rabbi Meir, who miraculously sensed what had happened and addressed the group: "Is there any among you who know the incantations for curing eye disease?" (These included spitting in the eye of the afflicted.) The group pushed the troubled lady forward, but she protested that she had no such expertise. Nevertheless, Rabbi Meir insisted that she spit in his eye seven times, after which he would be healed. She followed his instructions and then returned to her husband. Rabbi Meir's students were scandalized for they felt that the Torah had been disgraced through this treatment of a distinguished teacher of Torah. Rabbi Meir countered that his behavior followed divine precedent, for peace between husband and wife is not to be taken lightly.[42] We could attack the despicable behavior of that husband. Rabbi Meir could have done that as well. He chose to deal with the given, and he went to great lengths in his pursuit of restoring peace to a wife with her husband.

This was a favorite saying of Abaye of third- and fourth-century Babylonia:

A man should always be cunning in finding new ways of showing the fear of heaven. A soft answer turns away wrath (Prov. 15:1), and one should always strive for peace with his brethren, with his relatives and indeed with everyone, even with the non-Jew in the street, so that he may be beloved on high and well-liked below, acceptable to his fellow creatures.[43]

There are entire passages and lists of passages that I could bring to your attention dealing with the application of this principle to specific conduct with Jews and with non-Jews. The regulations and suggestions flow from the concept that the entire Torah was given for the sake of peaceful ways (*darkhei shalom*), as it is written, "Her ways [the Torah's] are pleasantness and all her paths are peace" (Prov. 3:17).[44] That verse from Proverbs is recited in the synagogue at the conclusion of the Reading of the Torah, after the Torah Scroll has been returned to the Ark.

Another section could be devoted to the thoughts of Jews concerning Jerusalem and peace. I limit myself to two sources. The rabbis taught that God comforts Jerusalem only with peace.[45] Jewish sentiments about Jerusalem are articulated in one of the early statements about it found in Psalm 122: "Pray for the peace of Jerusalem. May those who love you prosper. May there be peace within your precincts, serenity within your palaces. For the sake of my comrades and companions I pray that peace be yours. For the sake of the Lord our God I shall seek your welfare." These verses appear in a passage that concludes the talmudic tractate on prayer (*Berkakhot*), a passage included in prayer books toward the conclusion of services, before recitation of a prayer known by its first Hebrew word, *'Aleinu*, a prayer articulating ultimate allegiance to God alone and the hope that all humanity will turn from its various idolatries to that allegiance. Such universal acknowledgment would of course lead to peace.

To read all of the sources that I have quoted and to become immersed in their study is to be embraced by peace and tranquility, sustained by the comfort brought by these teachings and models for behavior. The basic problem with such reverie is the reality of so much of the world in which we live. The confession of that reality is contained in our daily newspapers. In the words of the psalmist, "Alas that I dwell with the ruthless, that I live among the lawless. . . . I am for peace, but when I speak, they are for war" (Ps. 120:5, 7).

One way of stating the problem that confronts us globally has been articulated by Abraham Joshua Heschel in a discussion on the meaning of having been created in the image of God:

> [This meaning] is veiled in mystery. It is impossible to say exactly what it means to have been created in the image of God. Perhaps we may surmise the intention was for a man to be a witness for God, a symbol of God. But instead of living as a witness, man, in so many ways, has become an imposter; instead of becoming a symbol, he became an idol. In man's presumption he has developed a false sense of sovereignty which fills the world with terror.

This type of affliction is not limited to leaders on the international scene whose decisions can determine the fate of many lives. It is found throughout our society, at all levels. A talmudic insight reads: "Ever since self-indulgence has become widespread, strife has increased."[46] Self-indulgence and self-aggrandizement are not motivations that lead those driven by them down paths of peace. Those consumed by ill will, bitterness, jealousy, and hatred may in their efforts attain a degree of satisfaction, but peace lies beyond their grasp, for they are unable to rise above their limitations, to reach beyond contention to contentment. Even the religious, whose pronouncements suggest that they should know better, are not immune to this affliction. Too often we see and suffer from the effects of God's cossacks, self-appointed and self-righteous, who rather than pursue compromise in the cause of peace pursue the compromise that places politics above principle. They are minutiae men, enlisting details in the service of their limited vision of what humanity can be. Their suspicion of others merges with a suspicion of themselves to form a callus that does not allow them to feel sensitivity for others or for the peace of the community. Such is the power of the pursuit of peace that it eventually will overtake them as well.

Dr. Louis Finkelstein continues the discussion begun in the Bible and perpetuated through ancient, medieval, and contemporary teachers and commentators:

> The Prophets of Scripture, struggling to overcome . . . divisions among men, found support for their plea in the unity of God, and the recognition that He is the Father and Creator of all mankind. . . .
>
> With astounding perversity, men have slain and tortured one another in the name of the traditions which declared them to be brothers, and used the Prophetic principle to create new divisions among themselves. In the mind of the men who could not attain the heights of the teachings of their own faiths, the command to love all men, became a command to love those who agreed with them, and to remain hostile and aggressive toward those who disagreed.
>
> Even when men did not use the Prophetic doctrine as a means for its own negation, they still did not let it interfere with secular aggression and hostility. Interstate and international conflicts continued; and were justified by the ration-

alization that the Prophetic doctrine was not of this world, but belonged to a distant Messianic age, to be ushered in by a divine miracle alone. In the present world, conflict was natural, and cooperation unnatural. Thus man could pray for peace while they prepared for war.

War is so unreasonable and wasteful a method of adjusting human differences that one wonders that men should have resorted to the hypocrisy of religious wars and the rationalization of secular wars to escape peace. No profound study of history is required to demonstrate that even judged by worldly standards the Prophets were right; and that man's happiness is dependent upon world peace. It is aggression that is unrealistic in terms of the present, and fantastic in terms of the future.[47]

In spite of and in the face of an often disheartening reality, Jews never despair completely. Jews live sustained by hope, prisoners of hope, looking forward to the reign of the Messiah, whose name is also peace.[48] Our rabbis have taught that when the Messiah comes to this world, he will begin by speaking of peace, as it is written, "How lovely on the mountains are the feet of the herald who comes to proclaim peace" (Isa. 52:7).[49] The Messsiah himself will be preceded by a herald, the prophet Elijah. In a discussion of Elijah's appearance, the rabbis of the Mishnah declare:

> Elijah will come neither to declare the clean unclean nor to declare the unclean clean, he will come neither to disqualify those who are presumed to be of legitimate descent nor to pronounce qualified those who are presumed to be of illegitimate descent; but Elijah will come to bring peace to the world, as it is written, "Behold I send to you the prophet Elijah . . . and he shall turn the hearts of the fathers to the children and the hearts of the children to their fathers" (Mal. 3:23-24).[50]

This vision holds such hope because it is beyond squabbles, beyond final pronouncements of who is preferable to whom. The yearning for peace will pull us above pettiness, together with all who care to join, for only a world in such a state will be deserving of the Messiah. The promise that he brings will be delivered finally to all humanity by him whose name is peace.

Listen now to a prayer attributed to Rabbi Nahman of Bratslav:

> May it be Your will, Lord our God and God of our ancestors, Master of Peace, King who possesses Peace, to grant peace to Your people Israel. And may that peace increase until it extends to all who inhabit the world, so that there is no hatred, jealousy, strife, triumphalism or reproach between one person and another, so that only love and peace will embrace them all.[51]

NOTES

1. Shabbat 10b.
2. H. L. Ginsberg, in *Encyclopedia Judaica*, vol. 13, pp. 194-96.
3. George Foote Moore, *Judaism*, vol. 2, p. 195.
4. *Ethics of the Fathers*, 1:18.
5. Palestinian Talmud, *Taanit* 4:2.
6. *Sifre, Naso* 42.
7. *Sifre, Bhukotai* 26.
8. Mishnah *Sanhedrin* 4:5.
9. *Sanhedrin* 38a.
10. Gen. Rabbah 4:8.
11. *Rosh Hashanah* 23b, Deut. Rabbah 5:12.
12. Lev. Rabbah 9:9, Gen Rabbah 12:7.
13. Lev. Rabbah 9:9.
14. Mishnah of Rabbi Eliezer, chap. 4, p. 85 in the Enelow edition.
15. Num. Rabbah 11:7, 16; *Sifre, Naso* 42.
16. *Sefer Abudarham Hashaleim*, p. 104.
17. Lev. Rabbah 9:9.
18. *Etz Yossef* on the priestly benediction, in *Otzar Hatefillot*.
19. *Iyyun Tefillah*, comment on the priestly benediction.
20. Num. Rabbah 12:4.
21. Deut. Rabbah 5:12.
22. *Iyyun Tefillah*, comment on *sim shalom*.
23. Y῾ *arot D 'vash*, comment *sim shalom*, in *Otzar Hatefillot*.
24. *Iyyun Tefillah*, comment on *sim shalom*.

25. *Dover Shalom*, comment on *sim shalom*, in *Otzar Hatefillot*.

26. *Iyyun Tefillah*, comment on *Hashkiveinu*.

27. Lev. Rabbah 9:9.

28. *Berakhot* 12a.

29. 1 Chron. 22:7-10.

30. *Semahot* 8, end; cf. Mehkilta on Exod. 20:22 and *Torat Kohanim, Kedoshim* 20.

31. Marcus Wald, *Jewish Teaching on Peace*, p. 156, citing *Sanhedrin* 27a. Rabbi Wald's volume (New York: 1944) is dedicated to the memory of his father Rabbi Jacob Wald of Cluj, Transylvania, who died as a victim of anti-Jewish riots on January 5, 1928.

32. *Tanhuma, Hukkat* 22; cf. Lev. Rabbah 9:9.

33. Derekh Erretz Zuta 11, cf. Deut. Rabbah 5:13.

34. Shabbat 63a.

35. Deut. Rabbah 5:15.

36. *Taanit* 22a.

37. *Likkutei Maharan*, section 1.

38. *Letters of Repentance*, cited by Arie Eliav in *Shalom* (Ramat Gan, Israel: 1975).

39. Ethics of the Fathers, 1:12.

40. The Fathers According to Rabbi Nathan, 12:3.

41. Ibid., 28:3.

42. Levi Rabbah 9:9.

43. *Berakhot* 17a.

44. *Gittin* 59b.

45. Num. Rabbah 11:7.

46. *Sotah* 47b.

47. Louis Finkelstein, "The Philosopher: Architect of Peace," from *Rab Saadia Gaon: Studies in His Honor* (New York, 1944), pp. 4-5.

48. *Derekh Eretz Zuta, Perek Hashalom*.

49. Lev. Rabbah 9:9.

50. Mishnah *Eduyot* 8:7.

51. Cited by Betzalel Landau, "The Anticipation of Peace in Hasidism," *Mahanayim*, no. 104, p. 166.

IV. Religion and the World: Conservation Ethics

INTRODUCTION

EDWARD KILMARTIN responds to the question posed in this case study first by delineating a scriptural view of the religious person's responsibility to and for creation as understood in the context of Christian tradition: that responsibility is rooted both in an acknowledgment of the Creator and in the perspective of the kingdom of God as the ultimate destiny of creation. A proper understanding of communal worship, Kilmartin argues, must take into account the interdependence of worship and social morality. Developments in the understanding of the Christian Eucharist, from the time of Irenaeus to the present, are surveyed with a view toward establishing the basis for a liturgical theology of social and conservation ethics. As in John Gurrieri's paper and the Catholic papers already presented, the Second Vatican Council is seen as a key moment of renewal of vision and hope for the church.

Jonathan Helfand "considers the work of God" from the perspective of Jewish tradition, both biblical and rabbinic. He notes the "three-fold guidance system" that the tradition offers the religious person in steering a course between "rigid traditionalism" and merely conforming to the passing fancies of the time in dealing with issues as popular and controversial as conservation. These three sources are woven together in his paper to provide a rounded view of basic Jewish principles operative in framing an adequate Jewish view of humanity's role in the maintenance and development of the environment.

Christian Worship and
Conservation Ethics

EDWARD J. KILMARTIN

THE MOST RECENT comprehensive statement of the Roman Catholic Church on the subject of the responsibility of Catholics in society is the Pastoral Constitution on the Church in the Modern World (*Gaudium et Spes*) of the Second Vatican Council.[1] Drawing on the various sources of Christian tradition, it offers much material relevant to conservation ethics. Direction is given for an approach to such questions as the care of the earth, stewardship of possessions, simplicity of life, and the problem of poverty. The relatively few references found in this document to the Catholic liturgical tradition should not be taken as an indication that its contribution is insignificant. In its own way the Catholic liturgy is a unique source for the formation and direction of a specific style of social behavior.

In this essay the theme Eucharist and Conservation Ethics is discussed with special reference to the scriptures. How does the liturgy of the Eucharist express what the Christian scriptures say on matters relevant to conservation ethics? Afterwards the problem of the personal appropriation of the liturgical message is introduced. The symbolic language and actions of the liturgy are open to a variety of meanings. Consequently the multivalent message is only partially received, in accord with the capacity of the recipient. The particular theological outlook and daily religious experience that participants bring to worship play a decisive role in the way the liturgical instruction is received. In this connection reference is made to the history of the practice of the Eucharist in the Western church. This shows that, for many reasons, the social dimension of the liturgy became obscured and so its effectiveness to contribute to the quality of ethico-social practice was impaired. Some of the significant changes found in the New Missal of Paul VI (1970) are cited as an example of the more balanced approach to the individualistic and social aspects of the Eucharist characteristic of the modern Catholic Church. The final section reflects on one important theological truth that must become alive in the consciousness of Christians and on the need for the experienced connection between worship and morality — if the liturgy of the Eucharist is to be an effective instrument of social change.

CHRISTIAN SCRIPTURES AND CONSERVATION ETHICS

The Christian scriptures witness to the creation theology of the Hebrew scriptures in which the human being, as crown of creation, is given dominion over all things of the earth (Gen. 1:26-27). Every aspect of life has meaning in relation to humankind. Even time, all time, exists for humankind: "The sabbath was made for man, not man for the sabbath" (Mark 2:27). An elitist conservationism, which would give preference to the preservation of nature over real human needs, is thereby rejected.

Moreover Christian scriptures interpret the phrase of Genesis "made to the image of God" to mean that humans are not like God simply in that they have relative dominion over creation. Rather it also implies that they are called to live a life of intimate personal union with God that expresses itself in their god-like generosity to others. Christians are invited to "Give to him who begs from you, and do not refuse him who would borrow from you" (Matt. 5:42; cf. Deut. 16:7-8; Sir. 29:1-2). This statement is made in a context in which Christians are told to follow the example of the Father in concrete acts of love toward everyone and so "be perfect, as your heavenly Father is perfect" (Matt. 5:44-48; cf. Lev. 11:44; 19:2).

The way of life advocated by the Christian scriptures entails the practice of inward freedom from possessions for one's own sake. Only through the practice of freedom from the impulse to consume, poverty of spirit, can one remain truly human in this world, submitting only to the God who cannot be identified with any worldly reality. Do not amass treasures that turn you away from God (Matt. 6:19-21). Do not identify human life with material goods (Matt. 6:25-35). Actual renunciation of possessions may be required to follow God's will (Mark 10:17-22). The teaching of the Christian scriptures is clear: the true disciple refuses to surrender to the merciless gods of mammon, power, or work; refuses to be inhuman and to contribute to the inhumanity in the world.

The intrinsic connection between the practice of inward freedom for one's own sake and the sake of others is also made in the Christian scriptures. Matthew 5:3 proclaims the promise of the happiness of the kingdom for the "poor," the *anawim* who lack material goods and stand in need of the blessings of God. At the same time this text highlights the inviolable otherness and absolute worth of all individuals before God. Elsewhere in the same gospel the consequences of this are drawn out. Matthew 25:31-46 affirms that faith in Jesus is the first step toward God. However, true disciples are manifested by the fact that they see Christ, the Son of Man, in the needy neighbor. All will be judged by what might not seem to be primary duties — that is, the corporal works of mercy. Attending to the real needs of others is the way to love God.

The teaching on inward freedom from possessions does not mean that Christians are called on to renounce, in principle, all possessions and consumption. Rather it renders a judgment on those who take part in the cult of consumerism. And it denounces an important source of this cult: the application of the law of uncontrolled economic growth and its promotion through the mass media.

From the point of view of Christian scriptures the most insidious effect of the application and promotion of this law is not the unnecessary consumption of material resources and the accompanying pollution of the environment. Rather it is the effect on human self-understanding. The promotion of this law leads persons to identify themselves with what they possess and to be inclined to derive life from industrial products. It threatens the creative and spiritual capacity of beings made to the image of God.

Christian scriptures also have something to say about the responsibility of Christians to work for the transformation of society. The apostle Paul places great stress on the final restoration of all things in Christ. He looks to the future solidarity of the human and subhuman world (Rom. 8:19-33). But he also says that Christians share by faith and hope in the final triumph over the disruptive effects of evil, a triumph already anticipated in Christ. They already dominate the world and its happenings (1 Cor. 3:21-22). This implies that Christians have the responsibility to provide a visible anticipation of the true life of the kingdom.

According to Mark 15:16, Christians are sent to preach the gospel "to the whole of creation," with the promise that it will be accompanied by visible signs of the future reconciliation of humankind and the material world. But the so-called subversive texts of the Christian scriptures point more directly to the responsibility of Christians to change society and its relationship to the material world. The parable of Matthew 20:1-16 can serve as an example.

In this pericope the situation of the kingdom of God is contrasted with that of a consumer oriented, efficiency oriented, society. Drawing on the world of work, this parable traces the movement from human relationships based on wages to one grounded on a relationship that transcends individualism and collectivism. In accord with the prevailing social custom, the vineyard owner makes a contract with workers early in the morning. He returns to the marketplace four times during the day to hire others. In the evening he pays those who came at the eleventh hour first and then those who worked longer. Each one receives the same wages. The laborers who worked all day complain, but not because they were paid last or because they receive less than what they had agreed on. They object to the owner's making the latecomers "equal to us." The owner's conduct was an attack on the barter system and the order of performance-reward derived from it. The protestors defend themselves by appealing to the system that gives them security on the basis of production.

These laborers, in the interest of economic identity, seek to remove others from their privileged place. But this results in effectively separating themselves from their fellowmen and losing the affection of the owner, who distances himself from them by a formal dismissal (v. 14). In addition the protestors negate the possibility of cultivating a higher form of self-identity.

This parable describes how the new situation of the kingdom of God involves an unexpected gift that comes to all. Those who work the least are the best example of it. They receive the same goods and the same love as do the others. In this new situation order of rank, inequality of income, and competition that destroys communication no longer exist. While it points to the joys of the fulfilled kingdom, the parable also alludes to the need for change in existing social relations, values, and norms. It does not call for total elimination of the lord-servant relationship, but points out deficiencies of the existing order.

This text can provide Christians with grounds for their struggle to overcome an economic system that causes divisions among persons. However, it also shows how ambivalent the wage struggle can be. It shows that it needs a deeper basis of solidarity if it is not to become an instrument of separation. The text does not furnish the basis for justification of particular political strategies. But, by the same token, it is an invitation to those who are ready to draw out the political consequences of partiality shown to the poor and suppressed classes.

THE EUCHARIST AND CONSERVATION ETHICS

In its own way the liturgy of the Eucharist trains Catholics for a critical response to the problems of conservation ethics — a response that corresponds to the orientation of the Christian scriptures. An analysis of some aspects of this celebration can serve as an illustration.

The use of the cosmic elements of bread and wine as medium of communion with God in Jesus Christ through the Holy Spirit should generate respect for the cosmos. The prayer of praise and thanksgiving made to the Creator of the world, when its meaning is fully appropriated, can have the same effect. The confession of the real presence of the Lord who died and rose from the dead, together with the proclamation of the hope of the resurrection from death of all humankind, should instill a profound respect for the human body.

This liturgy can also serve as a remedy for overcoming the dichtomy between person and community. It protests in a very explicit way against the temptation to define oneself over against others. Participants are identified as members of Christ and members of one another under the one Father, especially through the Eucharist. Through this conscientization individualism is transcended as well as narrow forms of collectivism. The emergent understanding of the human person and of world community offers the basis and source for moral living and analysis. It should not be neglected in an approach to problems of distribution and conservation of material resources.

The kingdom motif of the Eucharist reveals the social and cosmic range of Christian living. This liturgy constitutes a symbolic realization of the inbreaking of the kingdom of God, in which person, community, and cosmos are to realize their final transformation. It announces that all historical realizations of that kingdom are signs of the final consummation that will be achieved at the end of history. At the same time it challenges Christians to extend what happens in the liturgy to daily life: to make the coming kingdom present, by way of anticipation, through their activity in the whole range of social relationships.

Finally the implications of the sacrificial dimension of the Eucharist must be mentioned. In this liturgy the church recalls how Jesus dedicated his whole person and work to the mission he received from the Father. Inasmuch as his mission was to reveal the Father's love for the world and the way of access to the Father, his self-offering in loving obedience—even to death on a cross—reveals both the love of the Father for the world and the response that Christians are to make to the initiative of the Father. The former aspect is very poignantly expressed in Romans 8:31-32: "If God is for us, who can be against us? Is it possible that he who did not spare his own Son but handed him over for the sake of us all will not grant us all things besides?" The latter aspect—the Christian response to the Father's initiative—is brought out in John 14:6: "I am the way, and the truth, and the life; no one comes to the Father but through me."

However, through the eucharistic prayer the church does more than simply recall the self-offering of Jesus in thanksgiving. It also engages itself in a corresponding self-offering to the Father in union with the risen Lord. It enters into the movement of the Son to the Father in hope and trust. At the same time it opens itself in the Spirit to the self-communication of the Father not only for its own sanctification but also for that of others. Therefore participants commit themselves to employ their lives for others in order that the loving Father may be revealed to the world through their activity.

The eucharistic celebration is a symbolic playing out of the Christian commitment to be holy as Jesus is holy. Jesus is called "the Christ," the anointed one. He was set apart to give glory to the Father: "The child . . . will be holy" (Luke 1:35). Of himself he states: "For their sake I consecrate myself"—that is, he dedicates himself to the work of the salvation of the world. For he knows that he is the one "whom the Father has consecrated and sent into the world" (John 10:36). Because he is "the holy one of God" (Mark 1:24; Luke 4:34), his disciples must be holy: "But as he who called you is holy, be yourselves holy in all your conduct" (1 Pet. 1:5).

The dedication to holiness, which is made in the Eucharist, should have a profound influence on the Christian's attitude to the whole of creation. It is the expression of a willingness to serve God that is fully realized by letting God be God in one's life, providing God access to other human beings by one's lov-

ing service and by the employment of the whole of creation as
a gift of God to be used in the way he intended. In the "holy
sacrifice of the Mass" the community affirms that nothing is
profane; that all belongs to God and must be consecrated to his
service. This solemn liturgical affirmation should find an echo
in the protest against the misuse of the cosmos wherever it occurs: in the profanation of the human person, of human labor,
and of the material universe. The full meaning of the
eucharistic consecration does not begin and end with the consecration of the bread and wine. It embraces the *pietas antiqua*
of pagan antiquity, for which all things were holy, and the
"*sanctum sacrificium* of Abel, Abraham, Melchizedek, and
Christ" to which the Roman Missal refers.

A second-century church father, Irenaeus of Lyons, provides
a good example of how one can draw from the Eucharist con-
clusions that are relevant to conservation ethics. In his *Adversus
haereses*, directed mainly against the Valentinians, he for-
mulates his belief that the earth, the flesh of humankind, and
the human nature of Christ are linked in a fateful unity.
Therefore he could evaluate the world only in a positive way.
As creations of the good God, the earth and the human body
are good and beautiful. The incarnation and resurrection of
Christ are proof that the material world and all flesh are not
only good but will be gloriously transformed.

In his view the earth and all things in and on it are assigned
to the use of human beings in order that by means of these
things they might serve God, erect their tent on earth, and help
their neighbors. Although all earthly things have their deficiencies and weaknesses because of the sin of Adam, this does not
mean that the world cannot become a better place now and be
completely renewed in the end. The anticipation and promise
of the final renewal is especially associated with the Eucharist.
The Eucharistic bread derives from "our earth" — that is, from
the same earthly substance as the human body. When it is offered to God in thanksgiving and receives the invocation of
God, it "is no longer common bread, but Eucharist, consisting
of two realities: earthly and heavenly" (*Adv. haer.* 4.18, 5).

Consequently Irenaeus can state that our bodies, derived from the same earth, are capable of incorruption. Through communion in the body and blood of Christ there is imparted the eternal life that is the pledge of the resurrection.

In the last chapter of *Adversus haereses*, Irenaeus draws this conclusion from his previous teaching: because we are real human beings, we ought to remain on the level of concrete reality and so make progress, and not chase after unreal ghosts (*Adv. haer.* 5.36, 1). Evidently this progress should be made in the direction of the kingdom of God. This kingdom is realized fully only through the gathering up of all things into Christ. Every dimension of life on earth, according to Irenaeus, will be taken up into Christ just as the fruits of the earth and the work of human hands — the "bread from our fields," as well as the flesh of believers — are taken up into Christ by way of anticipation through the eucharistic celebration. Irenaeus could have drawn the further conclusion, which he does not, that every instance of failure to respect creation, every type of estrangement and egotism, is a countersign to the Eucharist. Those who celebrate the Eucharist should protest against such conduct: in this liturgy they celebrate, anticipation and promise, the recapitulation of all things in Christ.[2]

THE NEW MISSAL OF PAUL VI

The history of the development of the understanding and practice of the Eucharist in the Western church, prescinding from similar developments in the East, shows that the social dimensions of this liturgy gradually took a backseat in favor of a more individualistic approach.

The causes of this development are many — interrelated and often difficult to define. Over a period of centuries, reaching a high point in the late Middle Ages, the relationship between the cultic and juridical aspects of the church became increasingly obscured. This was both nourished by and itself fostered a cultic ethic based, albeit in an unreflective way, on an impure/

pure categorization of reality. As a result the sacraments, including the Eucharist, were thought to be properly related to the church conceived as institution of salvation for the individual believer. A form of piety took hold that was preoccupied with personal salvation and diverted from change in the world. Hand in hand with this trend, the notion that God works not only in history but also through history—that is, through the actions of human beings in the world—received scarce attention. One exception to the rule was the theological reflection on the implications of the juridical aspect of the church. Because the church is a divinely instituted, juridical society, it was concluded that church authorities have the power to act in God's name in the secular sphere.

It goes without saying that in many particular instances the individualistic view of the Eucharist was overcome by the experienced connection between worship and morality. This is especially true of members of religious orders of men and women during the high and late Middle Ages. Moreover the spirituality based on the imitation of Christ, popularized by the Carthusians and others during the late medieval period, was calculated to foster in the laity a profound awareness of the social implications of the Eucharist. A good example of this is *The Life of Christ* of Ludolph of Saxony.[3] But on the whole the Eucharist was presented in theological treatises, in popular preaching and teaching, as an instrument of the institutional church. It was celebrated by the priest for the benefit of individual Christians and their concerns. And it was the occasion for the bestowal of spiritual blessings as well as temporal blessings on the church and the world. This theological point of view continued down through the nineteenth century. However, in modern times considerable effort has been expended by liturgists and theologians to correct this imbalance by emphasizing the social aspects of this liturgy. The New Missal of Paul VI shows the influence of this new approach.[4]

This revised rite of the Roman Mass reflects the concern to guide Catholics to a wider vision of their responsibilities in society. All traces of the tendency toward a cultic piety directed away from change in the world are removed from the prayers of the Mass. The advice "to look down on earthly things and love the heavenly" (*terrena despicere et caelestia amare*), inserted frequently in the Roman Mass since the seventeenth century, is not found. This phrase had the effect of promoting a cultic piety, especially because an important qualification in its original usage disappeared. The seventh-century Gelasian Sacramentary interprets the phrase to mean that one should look down on worldly things to the extent that they distract one from the true goal of life.[5]

In the new and revised orations after the communion service — prayers asking for the blessings associated with the reception of the eucharistic body and blood — the orientation is generally toward the Christian's service in the world. Thomas Krosnicki has analyzed the content of these prayers, which project the vision of the Pastoral Constitution on the Church in the Modern World.[6] Perhaps the best example of this new direction can be found in the postcommunion prayer "for the laity." It reads in part: ". . . we ask, Lord, that . . . your faithful whom you wish to assign to secular matters be strong witnesses of evangelical truth and render your Church continually present and active in temporal concerns."[7]

These prayers provide an example of how the liturgy may be used to contribute to the transformation of society. At the same time these revisions raise a further question. To what extent should the Eucharist be employed as the medium of critical reflection on the many causes that prevent Christians from experiencing the life of the kingdom, by way of anticipation, in the daily conditions of modern society? It seems appropriate that participants in the celebration should be made sensitive to the various socially conditioned forms of slavery and suffering that weigh down the spirit. Also, because the Eucharist constitutes a symbolic anticipation of the life of the kingdom, participants should experience hope through a conscious playing out of their liberation from oppressive structures. Here, of course, the use of contrived rites that appeal only to a few must be avoided. Both the deep reflection on the meaning of the

Eucharist and the display of a truly genuine community spirit, which makes each individual conscious of their personal worth, can do much in this regard.

The relationship between the two is well expressed by Paul in 1 Corinthians 11:17-34. In this passage Paul calls attention to an important cause of the defective structure of the Corinthian community. The Corinthians bring their individualistic style of daily living into the worship setting. Consequently their lack of community spirit in daily life is not overcome through the Lord's Supper:

> When you meet together, it is not to hold the Lord's Supper. For everyone is in haste to eat his own supper. One person goes hungry while another gets drunk. Do you not have homes where you can eat and drink? Would you show contempt for the Church of God, and embarrass those who have nothing? [vv. 20-22].

This statement implies that the ideal form of the true life is not attained, by way of anticipation, when the gathering of Christians serves to reveal inequality and to legitimate the superiority of those with means. Rather than being the practice of hope of things to come, the Corinthian Lord's Supper obscures the promise of the kingdom and promotes divisions in daily life.

Paul then goes on to introduce the narrative of the institution of the Eucharist (vv. 23-26). He does not intend to give information about the mystery of the Eucharist as something esoteric. Rather it is meant to be a conscientization. It is a word of judgment about the relationship between the rich and the poor at Corinth. It calls for self-judgment: "If we judge ourselves, we will not be judged" (v. 31).

The meaning of the Eucharist is used to contribute to the transformation of the Corinthian community. At the same time Paul implies that the eucharistic liturgy should be an exercise of the practice of the hope that it proclaims. The playing out of the ideal form of the life of the kingdom is naturally presumed to have its effect on the quality of the social life of the church at Corinth.

The Liturgical Expression and Experience of God as Lord of History

The potential of the Eucharist to contribute to the transformation of society requires further exploration and experiment by pastors and liturgists. Moreover Catholic systematic theology can contribute to this by providing a new theology of worship that would be more world-related and more grounded on a theology of the sacraments. It also has the critical task of evaluating the conception of God that emerges from the liturgical texts. In this regard it seems clear that if the liturgy is to be an effective instrument of social change, it must offer a vision of God as Lord of history that takes account of the twofold perspective of the Christian scriptures.[8]

On the one hand the scriptures take for granted that God graciously intervenes in the political sphere as well as in the daily lives of individuals. From this point of view Christian service in the world takes on the character of a preparation for God's intervention. On the other hand the scriptures also recognize that God works through history, that he has given meaning to humankind so that it can give meaning to the world. From this viewpoint the activity of human beings who seek to give meaning to themselves and others — to remove injustice and overcome all evil — is understood to be more than merely a response to God's word. Rather it is God who initiates this activity, both revealing himself through it and changing the world. Love of neighbor is seen both as a preparation for God's intervention and also as the shaping force of good. Its paradigm for Christians is the life and death of Jesus Christ.

Christian liturgy should keep alive both aspects of God as Lord of history: his working in and through history. In this way it both fosters the hope of the manifestation of God's power and stimulates participants to take action in the world.

However, this word of scripture and its liturgical expression will be convincing to the extent that participants experience what is proclaimed both in the liturgy and in their daily lives. There is an intimate connection between worship and morality.

The liturgy recalls that Jesus Christ is the well-beloved Son who was sent to reveal the Father's love for the world. Consequently it challenges the Christian to follow the way of Jesus and contribute to the revelation of the Father's love, to be an instrument of his access to others through their loving service. On the other hand, in the activity of loving service in the world, characterized by the affirmation of the inviolable otherness of other human beings, one is led to the source of otherness: the ultimate Other. Through the moral behavior marked by thanksgiving, awe, and respect for the other, one may experience the entrance of God into one's own life, as well as one's role of providing God with access into the lives of neighbors.

The experience generated by this moral activity corresponds to that awakening in the liturgical act of thanksgiving and praise of God that has the effect of committing the believer to social action so that God may gain further entrance into the world. Christian moral behavior is the fruit and the test of the authenticity of Christian communal worship. It also provides the proper preparation for the liturgy and nourishes it — prevents it from dissolving into empty ritualism.[9]

NOTES

1. Austin Flannery, *Vatican Council II: The Conciliar and Post Conciliar Documents* (Collegeville, Minn.: Liturgical Press, 1975), pp. 903-1101.

2. A.W. Ziegler, "Das Brot von unseren Feldern: Ein Beitrag zur Eucharistielehre des hl. Irenäus," *Pro Mundi Vita*. Festschrift der theologischen Fakultät München 1960 (Munich, 1960), pp. 21-43.

3. *Vita Jesu Christi: Ex Evangelio et approbatis ab ecclesia catholica doctoribus sedule collecta.* Editio novissima curante Louis Marie Rigollot, sac. (Paris: Victor Palme, 1870). Ludolph of Saxony (d. 1378) completed this work around 1350. It became a popular spiritual book, used throughout Europe for centuries. Its spirituality is based on meditation on the life of Christ that leads to an interior cohabitation with Jesus, and a daily life of the quality of that of Christ. In this Jesus-piety the various aspects of the liturgy are

associated with objects, persons, and events of the gospels. Hence they are consciously employed in the service of this "existential christology." The classic example of how this form of piety, which has deep patristic roots and is currently experiencing a revival, overcomes an individualistic view of the Eucharist is the life of Ignatius of Loyola. His spiritual diary, written between 1544 and 1545, provides ample witness. A translation of the extant remnants is found in Simon Decloux, *Commentaries on the Letters and Spiritual Diary of St. Ignatius Loyola* (Rome: Centrum Ignatianum Spiritualitatis, 1980), pp. 134-96.

4. *Missale Romanum ex Decreto Sacrosancti Oecumenici Concilii Vaticani II Instauratum Auctoritate Pauli PP. VI Promulgatum, Editio Typica* (Vatican City, 1970).

5. Thomas Krosnicki, *Ancient Patterns in Modern Prayer*, Studies in Christian Antiquity, 19 (Washington, D.C.: Catholic University Press, 1973), p. 59, note 13.

6. Ibid., pp. 54-64, 143-50.

7. Ibid., p. 144.

8. D. Power, "The Song of the Lord in an Alien Land," *Concilium*, 92 (New York: Herder & Herder, 1974), pp. 85-106.

9. Enda McDonagh, "Morality and Prayer," in R. W. A. McKinney, ed., *Creation, Christ and Culture* (Edinburgh: Clark, 1976), pp. 187-203. See also G. Wainwright, *Doxology: The Praise of God in Worship, Doctrine and Life* (London: Epworth, 1980), pp. 399-434.

"Consider the Work of G-d": Jewish Sources for Conservation Ethics

JONATHAN I. HELFAND

THE TALMUD tells the story of a farmer who was clearing stones from his field and throwing them onto a public thoroughfare. A Hasid (pious man) rebuked him, saying, "Worthless one! Why are you clearing stones from land that is *not* yours and depositing them on property that *is* yours?" The farmer scoffed at him for this strange reversal of the facts. In the course of time the farmer had to sell his field and, as he was walking on the public road, he fell on those same stones he had thoughtlessly deposited there. He then understood the truth of the Hasid's words. The damage he had wrought in the public domain was ultimately damage to his own property and well-being.[1]

For over a century now, the world — the Western world in particular — has turned a deaf ear to the warnings of the wise and pious against the abuse of the environment and the wastage of natural resources. Modern society, like the farmer in the Talmud, has busied itself with improving its own lot, paying no heed to the consequences. We have far surpassed our ancestors in the scope and impact of our destructiveness. Water, land, air, and the wildlife they support have been despoiled and depleted beyond reclaim and in a manner unmatched in the annals of human history.

In the 1960s and early 70s new voices were raised in outrage over this rapaciousness — voices demanding the protection and conservation of the environment. In the counter-cultural revolution the corruption of nature by the establishment became an "in" cause and the word "ecology" entered the new rhetoric. However, as a product of antiestablishmentarianism, the cause required a villain. And although for some it sufficed to place the onus on society at large, others focused on organized religion — in particular, the Jewish and Christian traditions.

According to Arnold Toynbee, the biblical tradition was the nemesis that modern society had brought upon itself. The pollution of the environment associated with the advance of the industrial revolution and the recklessly extravagant consumption of nature's irreplaceable treasures could all be traced to one cause: the rise of monotheism. The doctrine that placed one G-d above nature removed the restraints placed on primitive society by its belief that the environment itself was divine. Monotheistic impulses were no longer restrained by a pious worship of nature. The God of Genesis told humankind to subdue and master the earth, proclaiming human dominion over the natural world.[2]

As a historian, I know that this doctrine misrepresents the past; as a Jew, I believe that my tradition can furnish meaningful lessons to guide individuals and society, even on the issue of conservation.

Before proceeding, however, a caveat is in order. In dealing with a popular controversial topic the theologian, no less than the historian, must take great care. Too often the religious apologist's desire to conform leads to superficiality and even misstatement. On the other hand, rigid traditionalism can blind the fundamentalist to the realities of both past and present. In seeking to navigate a course between being *au courant* and *au contraire*, the Jewish tradition offers a threefold guidance system: Halakhah, Haggadah, and *Tefillah*.

Halakhah, from the verb "to go," refers figuratively to the rules and statutes by which one is guided. It includes not only the Jewish scriptures, but also their traditional interpretation in the literature of the "oral law" — the Mishnah, Talmud, commentaries, codes, and responses.[3]

Haggadah, from the verb "to tell," describes the vast non-juristic literature, including biblical exegesis, homilies, parables, and proverbs, whose aim is religious and moral instruction and edification.[4]

Finally, *Tefillah* is prayer. In his seminal work on Judaism in the early Christian era, George Foot Moore observes:

> The true nature of a religion is most clearly revealed by what men seek from G-d in it. The public and private prayers of the Jews thus show not only what they esteemed the best and most satisfying goods, but their beliefs about the character of G-d and His relation to them, and their responsive feelings toward Him."[5]

Tefillah also has a didactic dimension. Rooted in the halakhic and haggadic traditions, it embodies their spirit and can be a vehicle for educating the worshiper. Indeed, the verb for prayer — *hitpalel* — is in the reflexive mode, as if in praying, worshipers are also addressing themselves.[6] Obviously, when the Jew seeks guidance in practical issues it is primarily the Halakhah and sometimes the Haggadah that are the principal guides. Nonetheless, as prayer sensitizes the worshiper, it too can offer guideposts and direction to the seeking heart.

An examination of these sources reveals that Judaism does indeed have much to contribute toward the formulation of public policy on conservation. The lessons culled from these texts address themselves to three primary areas of concern: (1) To whom does the world belong? (2) What is the purpose or plan of creation? (3) What practical guidelines does Jewish tradition offer for formulating conservation policy?

PROPRIETORSHIP OF THE WORLD

The argument that the Bible gave humankind dominion over nature and the license to destroy it is based on G-d's placing all of creation in human hands with the directive to "master it"

(Gen. 1:28-30). However, it is quite apparent from the following chapter (2:15) that the human race was not given a fiat to destroy at will. G-d never fully relinquishes dominion over the world. In describing the laws of the sabbatical year (Lev. 25:23), G-d reasserts his proprietorship over creation: "for the land is mine."

This principle of divine ownership of nature is reflected in the Halakhah and *Tefillah*. According to the Tosefta, "Man may not taste anything until he has recited a blessing, as it is written, 'The earth is the L-rd's and the fullness thereof' (Ps. 24:1). Anyone who derives benefit from this world without a (prior) blessing is guilty of misappropriating sacred property."[7] The list of blessings based on this concept includes numerous specialized and general blessings recited over comestibles, and a host of rules and regulations regarding their application and priorities.

The realization that we partake in a world that is not exclusively ours receives expression in a haggadic interpretation of the phrase *yumat ha-met* (Deut. 17:6) — literally, "let the dead one be killed." The implied question, of course, is: How can a person be dead before being executed? The Midrash Tanhuma explains:

> An evil person is considered dead, for he sees the sun shining and does not bless "the Creator of light" (from the morning prayer); he sees the sun setting and does not bless "[Him] who brings on the evening" (from the evening prayer); he eats and drinks and offers no blessings.[8]

Thus, we are placed on the earth to "master it," but we do so, in the Jewish tradition, as a steward, responsible and answerable to the will of the Master and obliged to acknowledge G-d's proprietorship at all times.

THE DIVINE PLAN

The Talmud observes: "Of all that the Holy One — Blessed be He — created in His world, he created nothing in vain (superfluous)."[9] Nothing in creation is useless or expendable; everything manifests some divine purpose. It follows, therefore, that there is a divine interest in maintaining the natural order of the universe.

Several expressions of this theme are to be found in conjunction with the laws of hybridization and mingling (*kilayim*). "My statutes you shall keep; you shall not let your cattle mate with different kind, you shall not sow your field with two kinds of seed, you shall not wear a garment of wool and linen" (Lev. 19:19). It should be noted that this verse is posed between the commandment to love one's neighbor and laws about certain forbidden conjugal relationships, apparently indicating that the maintenance of the natural order, like the social order, was a primary concern in biblical legislation. An exegetical passage in the Palestinian Talmud epitomizes this teaching. Commenting on the opening phrase in this verse, "my statutes you shall keep," the rabbis define these statutes as "*hukkot she-hakakti be-olami*," "the statutes that I have legislated in my world"— that is, you may not disturb or disrupt the natural law.[10]

This theme is developed further in a thirteenth-century study of the commandments called *Sefer ha-hinukh*. Explaining the roots of this commandment against "mingling," the author says:

> The Holy One created this world with wisdom, knowledge, and understanding and formed all creatures in accordance with their needs. . . . He commanded each species to reproduce according to its kind . . . and not to have species intermingle, lest something be lacking in them and His blessings no longer apply to them.[11]

Humankind was therefore enjoined from undermining the work of creation by engaging in acts of hybridization or intermingling.

In a similar vein, the *Sefer ha-hinukh* explains the injunction against sorcery:

> . . . therefore we were commanded to remove from the world anyone who attempts this [sorcery], for he goes

against the wishes of G-d who desires the settling [of the world] in the natural order that was set from creation and this [sorcerer] comes to change everything.[12]

Judaism's concern with the violation or distortion of nature is demonstrated in a talmudic tale. A poor man's wife died in childbirth and he could not afford to hire a wet-nurse. A miracle took place and he developed breasts and suckled the child himself. Upon hearing this, Rav Yosef commented: "Come and see how great is this man that such a miracle was performed for him." To which his colleague Abaye retorted: "On the contrary, how lowly is this man that the orders were changed on his account."[13] Although undoubtedly sharing Rav Yosef's concern for the well-being of the infant, Abaye simply could not countenance such an unthinkable violation of the rules of nature.

OPERATIVE PRINCIPLES

Judaism's genuine concern for maintaining what the rabbis called *sidrei bereshit* — the orders of creation, the plan and intent of the Creator — is expressed in several ways. Juridically we may distinguish two categories: first, injunctions against the despoliation of nature and natural resources and, secondly, legal imperatives regarding the development and conservation of the G-d-given environment.

Despoliation

BAL TASHHIT

The Bible (Deut. 20:19) forbids the destruction of trees by an army besieging an enemy city. In the Halakhah this biblical injunction — known as *bal tashhit* ("you shall not wantonly destroy") — has been expanded to form a protective legal umbrella encompassing almost the entire realm of ecological concerns. These extensions affect three aspects of the law of *bal tashhit*: the situation, the object, and the method of destruction.[14]

Although the Bible literally applies *bal tashhit* only to military tactics, the commentaries observe that the choice of this situation was not intended to limit its applicability; the Bible simply cited the most likely situation in which such destruction might occur.[15] The Talmud applies *bal tashhit* to numerous nonmilitary situations. Maimonides, in his eleventh-century code, declares: "This penalty [flogging — the punishment imposed for violating this biblical rule] is imposed not only for cutting it down during a siege; whenever a fruit-yielding tree is cut down with destructive intent, flogging is incurred."[16]

The Halakhah also extends the compass of *bal tashhit* with regard to the object destroyed. Not only trees but "all things" are included by the Talmud under this rubric.[17] Specifically, the Talmud mentions the destruction of food, clothing, furniture, and even water as being in violation of *bal tashhit*.[18] The nineteenth-century code of Shneour Zalman of Ladi sums up the consensus of Jewish legal opinion when he rules that "the spoiler of all objects from which man may benefit violates this negative commandment [*bal tashhit*]."[19]

Similarly, the Halakhah extends the jurisdiction of *bal tashhit* to include indirect and partial destruction as violations of this principle.[20]

The moral, if not legal, implications of this analysis for the makers of social policy are wide ranging. We bear responsibility for the destruction — complete or incomplete, direct or indirect — of all objects that may be of potential use or benefit to humankind.

ENDANGERED SPECIES

Jewish tradition also addresses itself to the problem of endangered species. A Haggadah in the Talmud re-creates the scene from the ark and has the raven rebuke Noah, saying: "You must hate me, for you did not choose [to send a scout] from the species to which there are seven [i.e., the clean birds of which Noah was commanded to take seven pairs], but from a species of which there are only two. If the power of the sun or the power of the cold overwhelm me, would not the world be lacking a species?"[21]

This concern over the destruction of a species is also invoked by the medieval commentator Nahmanides to explain the biblical injunction against slaughtering a cow and her calf on the same day (Lev. 22:28) and the taking of a bird with her young (Deut. 22:6):

> Scripture will not permit a destructive act that will cause the extinction of a species, even though it has permitted the ritual slaughtering of that species [for food]. And he who kills mother and sons in one day or takes them while they are free to fly away, is considered as if he destroyed that species.[22]

The *Sefer Hahinukh* offers a similar explanation, stating that there is divine providence for each species and that G-d desires them to be perpetuated.[23]

This theoretical sensitivity for animal life is translated into popular custom in a most touching manner. According to custom, a person wearing new attire receives the blessing, "May they wear out and may they be renewed [i.e., may you get new ones]." According to some authorities, this is not to be recited in the case of shoes or other garments made from animal skins, because, by implication, it calls for the killing of yet another animal.[24]

YISHUV HA-ARETZ

Finally, two ordinances regulating Jewish life in ancient Israel offer further guidance and introduce a principle of fundamental importance to our topic: *yishuv ha-aretz* ("the settling of the land").

The Mishnah states: "One may not raise goats or sheep in the land of Israel," because by grazing they defoliate property and thereby interfere with the process of *yishuv ha-aretz*.[25] The same legal principle is invoked by the Mishnah in ruling that "all trees are suited for piling on the altar except for the vine and olive tree."[26] These trees represented the principal products of Israel, and the rabbis feared that permitting their use on the altar might lead to the decimation of the groves and vineyards, and irreparably damage the Holy Land.[27]

The operative principle in these two cases, *yishuv ha-aretz*, calls upon the Jews in their homeland to balance the economic, environmental, and even religious needs of society carefully, to assure the proper development and settlement of the land.[28] In its active mode it demands that specific actions be taken to promote the maintenance and conservation of the natural envionment.

Maintenance and Development of the Environment

The Jewish scriptures mandate the establishment of a *migrash*, an open space measuring a thousand cubits wide around the Levitical cities, to be maintained free of all construction and cultivation.[29] According to Maimonides, this applied to all cities in Israel.[30]

The reason, as explained by the eleventh-century commentator Rashi, is that the open space is an amenity to the city.[31] The need for such a provision is ultimately based upon the principle of *yishuv ha-aretz*.[32] The implication in this and in other such cases is that *yishuv ha-aretz* requires us to consider the consequences of our creative activities in the world, not merely to clear stones and build cities or to avoid acts of wanton destruction, but to maintain a proper balance in the environment, providing the necessary amenities while insuring the mutual security of society and nature.

A striking example of this principle in action is found in the fourteenth-century code of Jacob ben Asher known as the *Tur*. In discussing the "rights of preemption" that a farmer has to his neighbor's property, the *Tur* notes that these rights are suspended if the purchaser acquired the land for the purpose of building a house and the owner of the adjacent field wants the land for sowing, because there is a greater *yishuv ha-olom* (settlement of the world) accomplished by building houses than by sowing. However, if the neighbor wishes to plant trees, he can remove the purchaser, because trees are more important for *yishuv ha-olom* than are houses.[33]

Several observations regarding this passage are in order. First, the *Tur* has applied the term *yishuv ha-olom* instead of *yishuv ha-aretz* (settling the land of Israel) to this case, thereby extending the concept and its legal application beyond the borders of the land of Israel.[34] Nor is Rabbi Jacob ben Asher the only authority to apply the restrictions and imperatives derived from the principle of *yishuv ha-aretz* to the whole world. For example, the eighteenth-century scholar Rabbi Jacob Emden also applies the concept of *yishuv ha-aretz* to a situation arising in Germany, concluding that even in cases where a destructive act is for sacred purposes, and therefore not in violation of *bal tashhit*, considerations of *yishuv ha-aretz* may render it illegal.[35]

In practical terms, this legislation indicates that there is no immutable schedule of priorities in dealing with environmental issues. Each case or problem must be examined according to the needs and ultimate goals of human society — the preservation and security of the "orders of creation." Furthermore, the *Tur* makes it clear that it is the responsibility of the legal authorities (in this case the Jewish courts) to intercede and even to interfere with personal privileges and individual rights to protect society and to conserve the natural order.[36]

Another Halakhah that is germane to the question of conservation is the ordinance of the sabbatical year (Lev. 25:1-7). Maimonides in his *Guide to the Perplexed* explained that the purpose of the sabbatical year is to "increase the produce of the land and to strengthen the soil."[37] The importance of such soil conservation is further emphasized in the following legislation.

In ancient Israel a special ruling prohibited plowing from passover of the sixth year, and certain other agricultural activities from the Feast of Weeks. The *tanna* Rabban Gamliel repealed this law for fear that the soil would be damaged if it remained unplowed for eighteen months.[38] According to one modern writer, it may be that an ecological change took place at that time as a result of the lowering of the water table, requiring further tilling of the soil to assist in water penetration.[39]

We have, thus far, seen how the Jewish tradition, in its various manifestations, has attributed proprietorship of the world to G-d, declared the maintenance of the "order of creation" a religious principle, and translated it into legislation proscribing the destruction of the natural environment on the one hand, and requiring the conservation and maintenance of it on the other.

In closing, I should like to confine my remarks to the two protagonists in the ecological drama: nature and humankind.

Although nature has indeed been, to use Weber's term, "disenchanted" by the biblical creation epic, it is wrong to conclude that by releasing humankind from primitive constraints, monotheism has given us license or incentive to destroy. In the Jewish tradition nature may be disenchanted, but never despiritualized. For Judaism, nature serves as a guide and inspiration. "Bless the L-rd, O my soul," cries out the psalmist as he views heaven and earth and the wonders of creation. "How great are Thy works, O L-rd; in wisdom You have made them all; the earth is full of your possessions" (Ps. 104:1, 24). Even a cursory glance at the daily prayer book will reveal the depth to which the Jew is stirred by nature and recognizes in it a profound manifestation of G-d. The legal principles and moral imperatives to preserve and care for the environment first take on meaning for Jews when they rise and start their day, blessing G-d for the rooster that marks the passage from night to day. The morning service continues with blessings and Psalms to G-d the Creator, seeing in the natural world the spiritual sustenance of human faith.[40]

Thus, even in an asphalt jungle the prayer book keeps persons in touch with nature, teaches them to revere nature, and heightens their sense of dependence on nature. The pilgrimage festivals do not just celebrate historical events, but mark the agricultural cycle—spring, first fruits, harvest—even for the child who has never seen an orchard or walked in a field. The prayers for dew and rain recited on Passover and Tabernacles alert us to the needs of nature and to our dependence on the vagaries of rain, wind, and sun.

The praying Jew becomes suffused with the spirit of the Psalms he or she recites and comes to view nature as a living testimony to a living G-d. Says the Talmud: "He who goes out in the spring and views the trees in bloom must recite 'Blessed is He who left nothing lacking in His world and created beautiful creatures and beautiful trees for mankind to glorify in.' "[41] When persons pray, they admire, praise, and are inspired by nature; how can they wantonly destroy it?

Like the ancient farmer of the talmudic parable, modern society suffers from self-inflicted wounds. The reason for this suffering is perhaps best analyzed by the rabbis in the following passage from *Ethics of the Fathers* (a tractate of the Mishnah): *Ha-kin'ah ve-ha-ta'avah ve-ha-kavod motzi'in et ha-'adam min ha-olam*[42] — "Jealousy, desire, and pursuit of glory remove us from this world." Or, in the modern idiom, impulse-control breakdown, keeping up with the Joneses, and ego-tripping — these are at the root of our estrangement from nature. Judaism calls upon humankind to control its appetites. And this is perhaps the key to all conservation ethics.

In conclusion, I should like to refer to a Haggadah from which I have taken the title for this paper.

Ecclesiastes says (7:13): "Consider the work of G-d, for who can make straight what He hath made crooked?" The Midrash Rabbah to this verse explains:

> When the Holy One—Blessed be He—created Adam, he took him to survey all the trees of the Garden of Eden and said to him: "See how beautiful and superior are my works; and all that I created was created for you. Take heed not to corrupt and destroy my world, for if you corrupt it, there is none who can repair it after you."[43]

The message and meaning of the Jewish sources for those who set social policy is encapsulated in this midrashic admonition: "Consider the work of G-d, O man, for if you corrupt it there is none who can repair it after you."

Bibliographic References

In the early years of the ecology debate several essays were written on the broad topic of Judaism and conservation. The following selected list may be of use to those who wish to pursue the topic beyond the outlines presented in this paper.

Carmell, Aryeh. "Judaism and the Quality of the Environment." *Challenge*, Aryeh Carmell and Cyril Domb, eds. (London and Jerusalem, 1976), pp. 500-525.

Freudenstein, Eric G. "Ecology and the Jewish Tradition." *Judaism*, 19, no. 4 (Fall, 1970), pp. 406-14.

Gordis, Robert. "The Earth is the Lord's — Judaism and the Spoliation of Nature." *Keeping Posted*, 16, no. 3 (December, 1970), pp. 5-9.

Helfand, Jonathan I. "Ecology and the Jewish Tradition: A Postscript." *Judaism*, 20, no. 3 (Summer, 1971), pp. 330-35.

Lamm, Norman. "*Al ha-aretz ha-tovah.*" *Hadoar*, 49, no. 28 (June 5, 1970), pp. 486-87. English translation in his *Faith and Doubt* (New York, 1971) under the title "Ecology in Jewish Law and Theology."

Pelcovitz, Ralph. "Ecology and Jewish Theology." *Jewish Life*, 37, no. 6 (July/August, 1970), pp. 23-32.

Rackover, Nahum. "Protection of the Environment in Hebrew Sources." (in Hebrew) *Dine Yisrael* 4 (1973), pp. 6-25. (Originally commissioned as part of a series of studies in Jewish law for the Ministry of Justice in Israel.)

Notes

1. *Tosefta, Bava Kama* 10:2. Cf. *Bava Kama* 50b.

2. Arnold Toynbee, "The Genesis of Pollution," *New York Times*, Sept. 16, 1973, section 4, Op-Ed page. This essay was based on an article that appeared in *Horizon Magazine* at that time.

3. For an excellent sketch of the literature of the Halakhah see David M. Feldman, *Marital Relations, Birth Control, and Abortion in Jewish Law* (New York, 1974), pp. 3-18.

4. George Foot Moore, *Judaism in the First Centuries of the Christian Era* (New York, 1971, repr.), vol. 1, pp. 161-63.

5. Ibid., vol. 2, p. 212.

6. Rabbi Samson Raphael Hirsch in his commentary to Psalms 5:3

and 32:6 emphasizes that the process of prayer entails self-cognition on the part of the worshiper.

7. *Tosefta, Berakhot* 4:1.

8. *Tanhuma, Berakha*, section 7. This theme is particularly stressed in the liturgy for New Year's Day, which, according to tradition, is not only the day of Judgment but also the anniversary of creation.

9. *Shabbat* 77b.

10. *Kilayim*, 1:7. Cf. the tanaitic midrash to Leviticus, *Sifra*, same passage.

11. *Sefer Ha-hinukh*, no. 244. Maimonides, recognizing the source of this law in the "natural order," rules that this prohibition applies to Gentiles, as well in the cases of grafting and interbreeding. *Mishneh Torah*, Laws of Kings 10:6.

12. *Sefer Ha-hinukh*, no. 62.

13. *Shabbat* 53b.

14. For a detailed discussion of these laws see *"Bal tashhit,"* *Encyclopedia Talmudit*, vol. 3 (Jerusalem, 1963), pp. 335-37. Also see Jonathan I. Helfand, "Ecology and the Jewish Tradition," *Judaism*, 20, no. 3 (Summer 1971), pp. 331-33.

15. See, for example, the commentary *Da῾ at Zekenim mi-ba 'alei Ha-tosefot* to Deut. 20:19.

16. *Mishneh Torah*, Laws of Kings 6:8. See also the *Kesef Mishneh* (commentary to Maimonide's code), ad loc.; *Sefer Mitzvot Gadol* [= *SeMaG*]. Negative Commandment no. 229; and Rabbi David Kimhi's commentary to 2 Kings 3:19.

17. *Bava Kama* 91b. Some commentaries, however, interpret it as meaning "all *trees*."

18. *Shabbat* 140b; *Kiddushin* 32a; *Shabbat* 129a; *Yevamot* 11b. In the latter case the text reads: "A man should not pour the water out of his cistern while others may require it." The *SeMaG* interprets this as being based on the law of *bal tashhit.* — On the question of the pollution of water resources, see Nahum Rackover, "Protection of the Environment in Hebrew Sources," (in Hebrew) *Dine Yisrael*, 4 (1973), pp. 18-19.

19. *Shulhan Arukh Ha-rav*, "Hilkhot Shmirat ha-guf ve-nefesh," par. 14.

20. The *Sifri* (a tanaitic midrash) to Deut. 20:19 includes the cutting off of water supplies to trees as a violation of the rule. Similarly, Maimonides, *Mishneh Torah*, "Laws of Kings" 6:8. Incomplete destruction is cited by the Talmud in *Kiddushin* 32a (see Rashi, ad loc.) and *Bava Kama* 91b.

21. *Sanhedrin* 108b.

22. Nahmanides, commentary to Deut. 22:6. See also his comments in Lev. 19:19, on the laws of *kilayim*: "He who mixes kinds denies and confounds the act of creation." These comments contrast with and undoubtedly modify his statements in Gen. 1:26, 28, regarding human mastery over creation.

23. Nos. 294, 545.

24. *Shulhan 'Arukh, 'Orah Hayyim* 223:6. On the Jewish attitude toward hunting and killing for sport, see Sidney B. Hoenig, "The Sport of Hunting: A Humane Game?," *Tradition*, 11, 3 (Fall 1970), pp. 13-21.

25. *Bava Kama* 79b and Rashi, ad loc.

26. *Mishnah Tamid* 2:3.

27. *Tamid* 29b: Maimonides, *Mishneh Torah*, "Laws of Things Banned from the Altar" 7:3.

28. This principle is also invoked in numerous other instances. For a review of this literature, see the *Encyclopedia Talmudit*, vol. 2 (Jerusalem, 1956), pp. 225-26.

29. Num. 35:2-5.

30. *Mishneh Torah*, "Laws of Sabbatical and Jubilee Years" 13:5.

31. See the commentary of Rashi to Num. 35:2 and to *Arakhin* 33b.

32. *Encyclopedia Talmudit*, vol. 2, p. 226.

33. *Tur Hoshen Mishpat*, par. 175. (Based on *Bava Metzi'ah* 108b.)

34. Ibid. See *Bet Yosef* (commentary of Rabbi Joseph Karo), no. 43, and the comments of *Prishah* to this paragraph of the *Tur*.

35. *She'ilat ya'avetz*, part 1. responsum 76.

36. *Bet Yosef* and *Prishah*, as cited in note 35, above. See also *Shulhan Arukh, Hoshen Mishpat* 175:26 and the commentaries there.

37. Part 3, chap. 39. Others reject this explanation, seeing this legislation as having primarily a religious and social function, not an agricultural one.

38. *Mo'ed Katan* 3b, and *Tosefot*, s.v. *kol*.

39. Rabbi Aryeh Carmell, "Judaism and the Quality of the Environment," *Challenge*, Aryeh Carmell and Cyril Domb, eds. (London and Jerusalem, 1976), pp. 512-13.

40. *Daily Prayer Book*, Philip Birnbaum, ed. (New York, 1977), pp. 15, 51 ff.

41. *Berakhot* 43a.

42. *Pirke Avot* (Ethics of the Fathers) 4:21.

43. *Koheleth Rabbah* 7.

V. Assessment

INTRODUCTION

IN THIS FINAL SECTION two major liturgical scholars assess the significance of views offered in the present volume and offer some trenchant insights of their own.

Pointing to the necessity for a "translation grammar" to make possible the internalization of each other's liturgical language in such exchanges, Lawrence Hoffman explores Jewish textual bases for social action. In this enquiry, Hoffman distinguishes two kinds of value statements: those specific to a given moral decision or situation, and those of a more general or consensual nature. Jewish liturgical texts as he understands them are limited primarily to the latter category. They possess a value-orienting rather than a value-defining character. It might be commented here that a similar situation, as described in the Catholic papers, prevails in the Catholic understanding of liturgy as well.

In classic rabbinic tradition, Hoffman argues, there existed a "gap between ethics and worship," at least insofar as the perceived intent of rabbinical worship was concerned. In later periods, however, worship as a means to an ethical end came to be stressed, along with the more traditional notion of worship as an end in itself. For these later Jewish authorities, prayer became "a religious obligation intended to generate a better world." Hoffman traces this intentionality of prayer through the philosophical school represented by Moses Maimonides and the mystical tradition represented by sixteenth-century Lurianic Kabbalah to the enlightenment views of modern Judaism. Again, it is of interest to note that in his Catholic paper arguing for a specifically ethical character for the liturgy (above), John Pawlikowski likewise stresses the medieval mystical tradition and moves from there to a consideration of contemporary attempts at liturgical innovation.

Gerard Sloyan's paper forms a fitting finale for this volume of prayerful reflection. It embodies the "other-directedness" of self-transcendence called for by the worship of a God who is wholly Other. Ironically, he notes, the very awesomeness of the transcendent Other establishes the basis for the Jewish and Christian "moral imperative" that the essays in this collection have noted in our liturgical systems. Prayer, in orienting us as community to God alone, enables us to acknowledge, and therefore to deal with, the injustices of the world. Although a good ethicist, he concludes, need not be a good liturgist, "a good liturgist *will be* a good ethicist." For in liturgy, the "holy God" approaches and calls his people to "do justice."

Liturgical Basis for Social Policy:
A Jewish View

LAWRENCE A. HOFFMAN

CATHOLICS AND JEWS have their own vocabularies. Chapters in this very book, for example, speak of "eschatological presence," and "charismatic healing [that] is not covenantal," and "Jesus, the creating and creative word of God [who] is also the word that forms history." Technically speaking, these utterances are "meaningless" to me. It is not a question of agreeing or of disagreeing with them. I simply do not recognize what it is that is being asserted and upon which I am to pass judgment.

My unfamiliarity with Christian language is not a small matter. Language, after all, reflects one's worldview by allowing some syntactical forms while forbidding others. Furthermore, it actually forms that worldview by defining for us the kind of world that must necessarily exist for our speech forms to be meaningful in the first place. Perhaps we require a "translation grammar" that would render the intensely specific "high context" statements of our faiths at least comprehensible to outsiders. At the very least, we Jews and Christians need great stretches of time together in which to internalize each other's existential basis from which our language flows.[1]

Particularly is this true of liturgy. In my interfaith discussions on the subject, I continually experience what I can only call verbal vertigo! I am continually on the verge of falling, because of the recurrent discovery that what I thought I understood, I do not.

Our conversations together approximate those featuring Shakespeare's fools:

> [Enter Viola and Clown with a tabor]
> VIOLA: Save thee, friend, and thy music: Dost thou live by thy tabor?
> CLOWN: No, sir, I live by the church.
> VIOLA: Art thou a churchman?
> CLOWN: No such matter, sir; I do live by the church; for I do live at my house, and my house doth stand by the church.[2]

I gather that Catholics have given a great deal of thought to what liturgy means. Jews have not. There is, in fact, no Hebrew word that expresses what the English word "liturgy" implies, except the modern derivative from the English, *liturgiah*, a word coined precisely because traditional terms would not suffice. Generally speaking, Jews have simply translated *Tefillah* (by which we often mean liturgical texts, and to which we have given much thought) as "liturgy," because (on the face of it) it seems to us that when Christians say "liturgy" they mean *Tefillah*. But we now discover that the word "liturgy" (for Christians) is just the tip of an iceberg that hides a mountain of theoretical presupposition. Questions about liturgy must certainly be Christian questions then, arising out of that presupposed theory.

But can they be Jewish questions also? And if so, should they? I believe the answer to both questions is affirmative, and my task here is to suggest why. I shall therefore ask: How (if at all) do value stances (I shall later explain this term) arise for Jews engaged in their liturgy? In answering this query, I shall try to define liturgy beyond its normal Jewish denotation of "text," but short of what I take to be a Catholic conception. And I trust my definition (tentative though it is) will do no injustice to Jewish experience. It might, moreover, have significance for Catholics too, though it is not for me to make that judgment.

Put another way, I want to summarize the subject of the

Jewish textual bases for social action, sharpening the focus to those bases that exist in the liturgical arena; and exploring at the same time what a Jew might legitimately mean by liturgy. That is, the existence of textual bases for social policies is, in and of itself, a fine thing, but I should like to enquire how it is that those bases function liturgically, if indeed they do function at all in the lives of men and women of faith who meet in Jewish worship.

My inquiry divides into several subtopics, and it might be useful if I summarize these in advance.

I distinguish first between two kinds of value statements: specific or substantive statements on the one hand, and general or consensual statements on the other. I will argue that liturgical texts tend to be limited to the latter, that they have no necessary consequences for specific social policies since they are too general, and that if we wish the content of the worship texts that we pray to be translated directly into policy statements, we shall be disappointed. I shall illustrate this thesis, to some extent, with material drawn from other chapters of this book.

This will lead us to the very idea that seems to underlie the initial conception of this volume: that prayer should have ethical consequences. We shall have to ask whether the idea is even tenable in the first place, and whether it is derivable from classic Jewish notions regarding the intent or purpose of prayer. We shall see that the way the question is formulated in this book's title, at any rate, betrays the fact that it is a response to post-Enlightenment conditions that demanded a justification of prayer in ethical terms. Post-Enlightenment Jews, particularly Reformers, but some Orthodox too, certainly, seem to have arranged their prayer books as if they believed that prayer should lead to specific ethics, that there should exist some immediate ethical payoff, so to speak, in the sense that we might expect the texts we read to be acted out in the personal behavior of the worshipers. But I shall conclude that in large part these modern Jews were mistaken. There is no liturgical and textual basis for social policy.

This is because the act of worship is not essentially a textual matter in the first place, and cannot, therefore, be reduced to the content of written assertions. As a matter of fact, we shall see that worship in the sense of liturgical texts acted out in the process of worship is ethically relevant, in that, although it provides no specific policy stands, it does create the readiness for ethical commitment, or what I shall call a value stance. I shall discuss this resultant value stance, tracing the notion back through the Enlightenment to medieval Jewish philosophy and mysticism. I shall conclude that there is a Jewish basis for social involvement, but that it flows from the act of communal worship and the consensual value statements as opposed to the substantive ones. So the liturgical basis for ethics is a general value stance. It will be transformed into specific policy pronouncements only after an extraliturgical process of debate and discussion that occurs totally outside the realm of worship.

Let me proceed then with the first part of my argument, the differentiation of two categories of value statements.

The study of philosophy and linguistics during the last half century or so has taught us to discriminate among linguistic forms. A very elementary dichotomy of form, it seems to me, is observable in the texts cited in this volume. Both kinds purport to adjure the man or woman of faith to act in such and such ways, to guide their behavior according to certain values or in the hope of attaining certain ends that are themselves held up as desirable. Let us call these two sorts of texts "value statements" and see how these value statements may be of one of two varieties.

In the first place, certain statements may belong to a rather general ethical rhetoric, the sort of thing to which one can hardly take exception.

These statements are, in a sense, classic distillations of religious wisdom, the crystalizations of millennia, axiomatic yardsticks by which one judges humanity. That some of them should find their way into the statutory prayers should come as no surprise, since prayer represents the codification of humanity's dearest aspirations, or at least the aspirations of those humans who still dare to aspire. That Christian and Jew should readily find parallel texts on such matters testifies both to our historical dialogue with each other and to the wisdom of the universal experience that the real world forces upon us all. I call these generalizations "consensual value statements."

Other texts, however, evoke no immediate nod of acceptability. They express less rhetoric and more substance. They lie within the corpus of tradition, untapped for generations, and then emerge as rediscovered concrete interpretations of the consensual texts already discussed. "Seek peace and pursue it,"[3] is an example of a value statement of the first kind (consensual). It evokes automatic consensus, but very little guidance for specific action. On the other hand, the notion that Jews should "choose select men to impose peace"[4] is a value statement of the second kind (substantive), calling for certain concrete policy guidelines. It is interpretive, open to argument, potentially capable of attracting parallel statements from the tradition that imply, or perhaps even say, the reverse. Such arguable propositions are substantive or specific value statements.

The issue immediately before us, then, is the selection of the category of statement that might best offer a guide to policy. If we choose the consensual, we attract no opposition, but formulate no clear notion of actual policy in the real world either. If we choose the substantive, we get clear guidelines for action, but no consensus on enforcing them. Ideally, we should like to discover substantive value statements that differ from most in that category inasmuch as tradition would be at least *relatively* unanimous in its support of the position they represent. We should then have specific guidance that though technically and theoretically open to refutation, is in fact never refuted in the tradition.

Have the essays in this book come up with any such substantive textual bases for concrete action? I think not. I shall not belabor this assertion, because I think it an obvious conclusion to the reader. Despite pages of careful scrutiny, we have discovered not one specific policy arising out of the liturgy. Regarding all three test cases — conservation, peace, and health — we cited a considerable number of consensual statements, and an equal richness of Haggadah (or associated lore) that might conceivably generate even more consensual liturgical statements. But few, if any, substantive statements have been found, and certainly none arising from the liturgy.

To reiterate, briefly: so far, our search for textual bases for social policy has led us to a variety of value statements that I divide into two categories: consensual and substantive. Only the second was sufficiently specific to suggest actual policies, yet there were few, if any, examples of the second that evoked automatic consensus. This left us then with the first, and raised the question of whether general notions, such as "Seek peace and pursue it," are in any way useful as guidelines for policy. On the face of it, the answer would appear to be no: policies are pragmatic; there are always choices between two or more optional directions, each claiming to fulfill the mandates of the generally accepted wisdom that the first (or consensual statements) represent. Now, it turns out that the texts of prayers almost always include only the consensual type, while the action-prompting statements, which are amenable to argumentation — that is, the substantive recommendations for behavior — are not found.[5] If, then, the consensual propositions are useless for policy-making, and if prayer contains only these, it might follow that prayer is a useless activity insofar as the creating of a textual basis for social policy is concerned. And here we run head on into a conflict with the prevailing notion that prayer is an ethical activity that has moral consequences. Indeed that is (as I said above) the very supposition behind the essays in this book. So let me spend some time tracing down that peculiar notion, in an effort to salvage consensual statements (of which liturgy consists) as a useful basis for policy, and simultaneously to validate liturgy as being of ethical consequence.

Where did we get the notion that prayer is ethically consequential? How old is the idea? Did the rabbis of the critical centuries when Jewish prayer took shape ever have the notion that the purpose of prayer was the fostering of ethics? Could they have imagined (let alone assented to) our quest for socially relevant textual bases in the corpus of prayers?

Despite various efforts to prove the contrary—the name of Max Kadushin comes most readily to mind[6]—I think the answer is negative. Though the rabbis of the Mishnah and the Talmud advocated both prayer and goodness, I do not think they prayed in order to be good. Nor when they discuss their being good, do they refer us back to prayers. The massive bulk of laws regulating worship seems unrelated, by and large, to ethics. My own view, though I will not argue it at length here, is that these laws are tied to cultic considerations. Prayer, or the offering of the lips, corresponded to the daily offering at the altar. The tractate on blessings was included in the Mishnah along with other offerings, the agricultural cycle of sacrifices entailed by the cult. Secondarily, I believe, these laws of prayer attracted ever more variations, as the system was honed to the fine point of perfection in which every conceivable possibility was explained. This fully elaborated system was intended as a disciplinary *regula* for a specific rabbinic social class, and eventually (not until the Middle Ages) was adopted as binding on all Jews.

The gap between ethics and worship is in fact enormous, a chasm really, in the mind of the rabbis. Though prayer might accidentally engender goodness, so too might any *mitsvah*, which we are told brings about other *mitsvot* in its train.[7]

Certainly this is so of the geonim, that age of Jewish authorities stretching roughly from the conclusion of the Talmud until about the eleventh century. It was these geonim who codified the synagogue service, giving careful attention to individual prayers and even specific words, and recording their considerations for posterity. Their criteria are many and varied: political, esthetic, theological, grammatical, exegetical, and homiletical. But I can think of not one extant case in which it is the ethical implications of the text that are the dominant (or even the secondary) concern.[8]

Even the recognizable rites that emerge from the high Middle Ages, the bases for our usage today, display a remarkable freedom of concern for the ethical implications of prayer. On the one hand, we see the same authorities who fix the liturgy being equally concerned about ethics; but on the other hand, they see no connection between the two realms. Eliezer of Worms, for example, is a noteworthy twelfth-century Jewish pietist. In his epic *Rokeach*, a compendium of law and custom, he reorders Jewish legal wisdom and introduces his magnum opus with a fervent call for repentance, while arguing continually that in ethics the Jewish saint must even exceed the letter of the law. But when it comes to deciding among alternative texts of prayers, he (and his school of decisors) utilizes such obscure notions as numerology—the mathematical sum to which the arithmetical equivalent of a word's letters will add.[9]

Moreover, we have in the traditional liturgy some very unethical statements, or at least statements that, however well they may be adequately explained away as reactions to specific historical events, ought not, from the viewpoint of universal ethics, be retained as guides for human conduct generally. I have in mind, for example, the first-century daily malediction against heretics, who, we are told, "should have no hope";[10] or the citing of scripture asking God to "Pour out Thy wrath on the nations that know Thee not," in the traditional Passover Haggadah. Interestingly enough, these and similar hostile reactions are generally not excised from the liturgy, even though (and this is the point) there is ample precedent: medieval authorities argue as a matter of course that prayer practices adopted under the stress of unusual circumstances should be dropped when conditions stabilize. Thus the principle of returning a prayer text to normal was accepted and even preached both by geonim in the East and by some European Jewish leaders in the West. But the precedent was not invoked to deal with ethical concerns!

Yet these same rabbis were far from lacking in ethical sensitivity. They wrote ethical wills,[11] and continually probed ethical implications of the Jewish way of life. They altered Jewish law dealing with Christians, for example, to reflect new, ethically advanced notions of a Christian covenant with God.[12] But they agreed with their inherited Jewish tradition in seeing worship as other than an exercise in better living. Whatever benefits might accrue to human nature as a result of worship were unrelated to that worship, because there was no inherent connection between prayer and human goodness.

Of course one prayed for goodness, for sinlessness, and the like. And at times, the confessional of Yom Kippur, for example, one pondered the implications of the detailed spelling out of ethical stances. But only rarely are changes in the worship text made as a result of a desire to couple prayer with ethics. Ethics is at best a by-product of prayer, and prayer for its part, maintains its own stubborn integrity as a religious discipline deserving of consideration in its own right.[13]

How, then, do we arrive at the popular assumption that prayer is good for us because it helps us be good? Rephrased, popularly, how do modern men and women develop the hubris to advertise, "The family that prays together stays together," as if staying together is the measure of praying together?

This attitude should be traced back in time to find out specifically when and how it arose. Even without such a controlled investigation, however, it should be clear that as widely as it is assumed today, this radical coupling of worship and ethics represents a disjuncture with the past. It certainly appeals to the heightened anthropocentrism of our time, and it preserves prayer as an efficacious human activity even in a world where the hand and voice of God seem painfully absent. It is no doubt rooted in the nineteenth-century critique of religion; an appeal to optimism, activism, individualism, and progress. As such, it appears most clearly in Reform liturgy, where old particularistic prayers are transmuted into clarion calls for ethical behavior and societal policies of benefit to all. But the same attitude can be found as well in Central European neo-Orthodoxy, where treatises on prayer or commentaries accompanying the prayer texts transform the words of worship in the same universalistic direction. To cite but one example, in 1836 the leader of German neo-Orthodoxy, Samson Raphael Hirsch, defined prayer as "the exaltation and sanctification of our spiritual life by symbolic words and acts, *to the end that our conception of our task may be rendered clearer and we be better fitted to fulfill our mission on earth.*"[14] Elsewhere he tells us that the Hebrew word "to pray," *lehitpallel*, really means "serious soul-searching."[15]

Whatever its provenance, this nineteenth-century liturgical

anthropocentrism may yet have some validity. To judge it as modern is not necessarily to declare it misguided, but only to point out that it is not the raison d'être of prayer known to classical Jewish sources. The putative connection between prayer and ethics will have to be examined further before we can pass judgment on it.

At any rate, the fact that this approach is still alive and well today is proven by the task set before the authors of the essays in this volume: the analysis of liturgical texts with an eye toward their forming bases for ethico-social policies. The question is whether or not this view now deserves abandonment, whether the search for necessary connective tissue between prayer and heightened ethical sensitivity will prove to be a mere chimera, an apologia for the spiritlessness of modern times, an idea from which we should rapidly dissociate ourselves.

The answer, I think, is that it depends on the connection we want to find. If we are looking for a direct cause and effect relationship between liturgy and policy, I am afraid there is none. The family that prays together will not necessarily stay together, or, if it does, the content of the texts for praying are not the immediate cause of their staying. That is to say, reading prayers about goodness does not necessarily teach us what policies to accept to make us good. The recasting of classic reform liturgy to include every conceivable bit of ethical advice did not by itself guarantee that entire generations of pious Jewish citizens would systematically hew to identical behavior policies with higher ethical implications.

On the other hand, those Reform Jews who prayed regularly did emerge with a certain developed ethical consciousness. If they were not good all the time, at least they knew from their prayers (now translated into the vernacular) that their religion called on them to be good, and that they had failed to meet the demands of the task. Their liturgy informed them that they had a mission, they were a chosen people, they were a light to the nations. "Why do nations lift up sword against nation," they read, or "The earth is the Lord's and the fullness thereof; the world and they that dwell therein. Who shall ascend the mountain of the Lord, and who shall stand in His holy place? They that have clean hands and a pure heart."[16]

The difference between their failure to be ethically good in every specific instance and their general commitment to goodness should recall to us the dichotomy between substantive and consensual value statements. We have noted that liturgy contains only the latter, whereas it is the former that lead to specific policy positions. Apparently those consensual value statements that characterize prayers, though giving little or no guidance for specific policies, can at least be credited with reenforcing a general state of moral readiness — that is, they create what I have called a value stance.

A value stance arises out of the interaction of worshipers with a text, during the act of prayer. Out of their commitment to praying together as a community that embodies certain traditions and attitudes toward the world, there are formulated not value statements, but a value stance. This arises from the fact that one identifies oneself with a certain *ecclesia* in the first place. The value stance takes the form of the totality of generalized attitudes reflected in the consensual value statements that are then appropriated by the individual as value perspectives common to all members of the faith community. It is in the act of prayer that these are rehearsed and internalized, as part of the social construction of reality.[17]

So there is some connection between prayer and ethics after all. It is not one that leads easily, immediately, or predictably to a series of ethically defensible postures in specific issues. But it can be said that the very act of prayer with its rote recitation of consensual value statements at least reenforces worshipers' commitment to a state of ethical readiness. Thus, in sum, worship defines one as a member of a group with a given ethical stance that can then be elaborated outside the worship setting into specific ethical policies.

We are left with saying that substantive value statements may indeed form the bases of social policy, when, following upon the liturgical affirmation of general values, they are successfully argued against other positions suggested equally by the tradition. But these substantive statements are not carried in the liturgy. The liturgy carries consensual statements, which, though giving no policy guidelines, do represent the valid role of prayer in developing ethical consciousness.

The experience of worship unifies group members by the ritualized presentation of a system of meaning that includes within it a value stance.[18] This value stance is encoded in the network of consensual value statements that members internalize as defining characteristics of their religious community and, thus, of themselves. They may still differ on policies, of course, because policies are derived from substantive not consensual value statements. And substantive statements, being nonliturgical and not part of the ritualized meaning system, permit argumentation and open debate within the context of the common value stance that both parties to the debate share. It is a value stance, then, that worship provides, through shared participation in even the most obvious truistic rhetoric; the unexceptional, taken-for-granted consensual value statement.

It must be emphasized that these consensual statements do not actually state anything, in the sense of making an assertion that is open to assent or denial. We are dealing not so much with words of a text as with the experience of those words when they are recited liturgically. Only fools (or, perhaps, scholars?) would attempt to read the paragraphs of prayer as if they were short essays of substance. It is precisely substance that must be avoided if consensual statements are to be consensual. So it is not the message of the words but the message of the medium that counts. It is the very *act* of worship that has ethical significance. The act presents a system of meaning that includes consensual value statements and, thus, obligates worshipers to a commonly held value stance.

I have argued against the simplistic view that the content of prayer texts, if ethical, promotes ethically sound behavior in specific moral dilemmas. On the other hand, we now see that prayer does promote a readiness to adopt social policies, the specific details of which are arrived at later, through a nonliturgical consideration of the substantive texts of the tradition. This is so because prayer provides a value stance. We saw before that the classic Jewish tradition is relatively impervious to the notion that the words of prayer should reflect ethical desiderata; but the notion before us now, that the very *act* of prayer has ethical importance, does appear in Jewish tradition.

Unlike the rabbis of the tannaitic and amoraic periods who (as we have seen) saw no necessary connection between prayer and ethics, later authorities most certainly did consider the act of prayer a religious obligation intended to generate a better world. In different ways, this belief goes back equally to the philosophical and mystical traditions. At issue is the difficulty I alluded to earlier: a difficulty endemic to our age, but foreseen by thoughtful persons in times past — that is, to put it bluntly, prayer is self-evident to those who presuppose the existence of a God who hears it. But if one's philosophy entails a different sort of God, or no God at all, prayer must be justified by recourse to some other notion that is not in question. The Enlightenment insistence that prayer texts reflect ethics, therefore, was related to a more general malaise that persons sensed regarding worship, stretching back to medieval ideologies quite diverse from one another, but essentially the same as regards the problem of justifying prayer. I have in mind the philosophy of Moses Maimonides (1135 to 1204) and that of the sixteenth-century Lurianic Kabbalah.

Champions of Enlightened Jewish religiosity had nothing but contempt for Lurianic mysticism, and they did it an injustice in not recognizing its philosophical basis. If Maimonides was the Aristotelian carrier of tradition (whom they duly idolized), the Kabbalah was inspired by Neo-Platonism, and deserved equal learned esteem.[19] Both philosophical systems shared with the Enlightenment the face that, given the cultural assumptions of their times, the traditional talmudic view of prayer was rendered unaccaptable.

We have seen how the Enlightenment justified prayer by seeing in it a means of forging a better world. But the Kabbalistic system too emphasized universal rectification (*tikkum olam*).

Like the moderns moreover, the Kabbalists said openly and expressly that prayer was not just one among many religious commandments (against the prior rabbinic view that did not discriminate among *mitsvot*); and they posited the existence of a secondary benefit of cosmic scope that made worship so significant. Both the Enlightenment and the Kabbalah felt the need, then, first to elevate and then to justify prayer. Moderns did so by adapting ethically rich meditations, translations, and commentaries. But Kabbalists too composed introductory meditations (*kavvanot*) to express the hidden purpose behind the manifest prayer content. So the mythological imagery of the Kabbalistic system, complete with emanations of divine light, alienation of sparks, and the like, should not blind us to its essential similarity to Enlightenment ideologies — Reform Judaism, for example. Both systems aim at world order and moral perfection, and believe that the act of worship will bring them about.[20]

They differ, of course, in that Enlightened Western religion emphasized the effect on the worshiper of the manifest prayer content, whereas Kabbalism saw mystical connections between the act of prayer — or the hidden levels of meaning behind the words and letters — and the desired end. But the end was the same. Only the metaphor used to describe it varied. Nineteenth-century German Jews tapped the cultural backdrop of European Romanticism with its faith in human potential, and its facile belief in history, evolution, and progress. Because science too adopted the same language of expression, it was inevitable that the scientific study of Judaism — not to mention ourselves, who are scientific scholars and children of the West — ended up viewing the Enlightenment metaphor as logical and therefore acceptable, while rejecting the Kabbalah as absurd fantasy. We even deny at times that our own metaphor is a metaphor, and thus fail to see that both mystic and enlightened Jew have at least this much in common: we both demand of worship not the selfish satisfaction of individual petitioners' requests, but the purging of evil from the cosmos itself.

As for Maimonides, simply consider his own testimony in his *Guide to the Perplexed*. When discussing the status of prayer as a necessary, though not a necessarily correct, belief, Maimonides describes "the belief that [God] responds instantaneously to the prayer of someone wronged or deceived" as being "necessary for the abolition of reciprocal wrongdoing":

> The end of these actions pertaining to divine service is the constant commemoration of God, the love and fear of Him, the obligatory observance of the commandments in general, and the bringing about of such belief concerning Him as is necessary for eveyone professing the law. . . . *These are actions which bring about useful opinions.*[21]

Shades of Emile Durkheim! For Maimonides, prayer is *socially* necessary; for the Kabbalists, it will set in motion divine activity designed to right the cosmic wrongs. For enlightened Jews it promotes ethical behavior, such that the authors of this book are invited to inquire about the liturgical bases for social policy.

I emphasize the fact that all three systems (though apparently diverse) are actually very similar. All treat worship, at least in part, as a means to an end; all see the desired end as some further state of mankind's well-being; and all cast that state of well-being into some specialized vocabulary with imagery consistent with their own unique philosophical languages. If we insist, then, that worship, as an act, has ethical consequences, we may not have the support of the earliest strata of rabbinic opinion, those worthies who still took worship to be an end in itself, mandated by a living God who listened to and answered prayers. But we do stand in the mainstream of Jewish opinion from the dawn of medieval philosophy and siding also with that most apparent of medieval creatures, Lurianic mysticism. The vocabulary of our precursors — active intellect, broken vessels, reparation of the universe, and the like — may not seem as congenial to our imagination as what we have called "bases of religious social involvement," but the intent is the same. The world has changed less than the metaphors describing it! We still live in a world sated with woe, crying out for Maimonide's "useful opinions"; for the kabbalistic freeing of the sparks and reparation of the universe (*tikkun olam*); or for our religious social involvement. We have rightly determined to consider the extent to which these things can be found in our traditions.

I argued at the outset that of two kinds of value statements, only consensual ones are liturgical. Though their liturgical recitation does not produce social policies, it does build what I call an ethical stance on the part of worshipers who internalize ethical catch-phrases and then meet in other arenas to spell out the specific consequences of their commitment to consensual general affirmations. There seems to be no immediate causal connection between the content of the consensual texts recited liturgically and the social policies adopted, since the policies derive from decisions dependent, among other things, on the second category of text, the extraliturgical, substantive ones. But we found a connection between the very act of prayer and a resultant ethical stance, and we traced this connection back to philosophical and mystical worlds of discourse.

The question put to me was: What are the liturgical textual bases for religious social involvement? The answer I must now give is that the most important such texts are not the texts at all, but the liturgical acting out of the texts in a community of worshipers. Prayer does have a social perspective. It fortifies us as a faith community to be committed to social involvement in the first place.

NOTES

1. This view of the role of language is derived from the linguistic tradition going back to Ferdinand de Saussure, and I borrow the terms "translation grammar" and "high context" from Martin Van Buren, *The Edges of Language* (New York: MacMillan, 1972) and Edward T. Hall, *Beyond Culture* (New York: Doubleday, 1977).

2. *Twelfth Night*, Act 3, Scene 1.

3. See above, p. 108.

4. See above, p. 110.

5. That newly created prayer books should deliberately be so was argued forcefully by Abraham Cronbach in "The Personal Aspects of Prayer," *CCAR Yearbook*, 57 (1947), pp. 379-388, and reprinted in

part under the title "The Language of Debate and the Language of Prayer" in Lawrence A. Hoffman, *Gates of Understanding* (New York: Central Conference of American Rabbis, 1977), pp. 41-45.

6. Max Kadushin, *Worship & Ethics* (Evanston, Ill.: Northwestern University Press, 1964.

7. *Mitsvah goreret mitsvah* (Avot 4:2).

8. These criteria are fully described in Lawrence A. Hoffman, *The Canonization of the Synagogue Service* (Notre Dame, Ind.: University of Notre Dame Press, 1979).

9. *Birkat minim*, the twelfth benediction of the *Tefillah*. See Philip Birnbaum, ed., *Daily & Sabbath Prayer Book* (New York: Hebrew Publishing Co., 1949), p. 88.

10. See Philip Birnbaum, ed., *Passover Haggadah* (New York: Hebrew Publishing Co., 1976), p. 52.

11. See Israel Abrahams, *Jewish Ethical Wills* (Philadelphia: Jewish Publication Society) and "Jewish Ethical Wills," *JQR*, 3 (1891), pp. 436-84.

12. See, for example, the discussion by Jacob Katz, *Exclusiveness & Tolerance* (New York: Schocken, 1962). esp. p. 115.

13. The best example of this position is the liturgy of the *yodei merkavah* mystics who left us with much that was to form the basis for rabbinic prayer of the first few centuries, including our "Holy Holy Holy," doxologies generally, and many of our basic blessings. Their liturgy, as Scholem noted, is essentially without any ethical considerations whatsoever: "The moral doctrines found in [their] literature are pale and bloodless," he declares. Though prayer is central in the mystics' world, ethics are practically absent, "alien in [the mystical] spirit," in Scholem's words. That Scholem should even search for ethics as a category of religious thought potentially imbedded in worship betrays his modern Western understanding of religion, in the first place. See Gershom Scholem, *Major Trends in Jewish Mysticism* (New York: Schocken, 1941), p. 79.

14. Samson Raphael Hirsch, "The Nineteen Letters on Judaism" (New York: Philip Feldheim Publ., reprint ed. 1960), p. 75; italics added.

15. Cited from Horeb. p. 618, by Noah H. Rosenbloom, *Tradition in an Age of Reform*. (Philadelphia: Jewish Publication Society, 1976), p. 379.

16. Citations taken from the *Union Prayer Book*, vol. 1, 1894; revised ed., p. 192, and newly revised ed., p. 194.

17. I borrow the term "social construction of reality" from the title

of the book by Peter Berger and Thomas Luckman, *The Social Construction of Reality* (New York: Doubleday, 1966).

18. My position is in accord, particularly, with Clifford Geertz who defines religion as "A system of symbols which acts to establish . . . moods and motivations . . . by formulating conceptions of a general order of existence, and clothing these conceptions with such an aura of factuality that the moods and motivations seem uniquely realistic" (Clifford Geertz, *The Interpretation of Cultures* [New York: Basic Books, 1973], p. 91).

19. I owe this realization, as well as the discovery of the Maimonides citations (below) to my teacher and colleague Leonard Kravitz.

20. Scholem has argued a direct relationship between the families who composed the most extreme Kabbalistic sects, the Frankists, and their children who pioneered Enlightenment and Reform. See, e.g., his "A Sabbatian Will From New York," Gershom Scholem, *The Messianic Idea in Judaism* (New York: Schocken, 1971), pp. 167-75.

21. *Guide to the Perplexed* 3.28; italics added.

Liturgical Basis for Social Policy:
A Catholic View

GERARD S. SLOYAN

REGULAR ATTENTION to the daily press or radio and television news makes clear the areas where the Jewish and Catholic communities work most vigorously to see that justice is done.

Jews seek peace in their homeland, the state of Israel. They look for an end to harassment everywhere, in large cities where Hasidic Jews live in concentration or in suburbs where synagogues are vandalized. They oppose quotas in hiring and professional schools, the "reverse discrimination" that mandates the preferential hiring of racial minorities.

In brief, Jews look for justice for their people in every case where political systems guarantee it but fall short in practice. They likewise are frequently in the forefront of efforts to gain social justice for others than themselves, a heritage of the teaching of the prophets and their own experience of injustice.

Catholics have overcome in many segments of life the prejudice of cultural ascendancy ("anti-Catholicism is the anti-Semitism of the liberal") and therefore tend to seek justice in matters such as the inequitable tax burden, as they perceive it, that results from conducting religious schools; hospital and health services where they are pressured to conform to a prevailing ethic on contraception and abortion; and areas of social injustice to Catholic populations such as Hispanics and

Haitians as once to Italians and Slavs. The consistent representations of the two groups have a *parti pris* character that is dismissed by the populace at large as special pleading or (in the Catholic case) a failure to be satisfied with the constitutional settlements arrived at by the majority.

The struggle for justice on a wider scale, as carried on by members of both groups, is hard to identify in terms of Judaism or Catholicity. One can try to identify the public figures who fight for justice by their surnames, but that is a chancy business. In the causes outlined in the two paragraphs above, the influence of rabbis, bishops, and priests is strong. Yet a case could be made for their being the led as much as the leaders, because it is doubtful that unpopular causes could flourish for long in either constituency. The prevailing currents are not easy to trace when it comes to seeking social justice for all, not just members of one's religious or ethnic group. This body or that, made up in part of identifiable Jewish or Catholic citizens, works hard to achieve good wages, hours, and working conditions, let us say. The fact is clear but the motivations are less so. Are these motivations religious, are they rooted in unionism, or are they the result of proximity to immigrant origins? Sorting out such factors is a subtle affair. What is to be made of the zeal for justice of the lapsed and alienated Catholic, the thoroughly secular Jew? Does this come as part of a religious heritage that cannot be suppressed or is it a response to omissions experienced in the tradition? Matters grow murkier when it comes to identifying those strugglers for justice who cannot be shown to have any familiarity whatever with forms of public prayer, so remote is the tradition in their background. One is thrown back on theories of race memory or unwarranted assumptions about the influence of the "old parish" and the high holy days. A solid, direct impact is hard to prove.

Religious sociologists are understandably chary about alleging influences when they cannot establish correlations. The safer technique is the nonscientific one of citing religious texts from the Bible and Talmud, liturgy and prayer book, and saying that they cannot *not* have had an influence on the lives of Jews and Catholics who are certifiable workers for the promotion of justice. The unreliability of analyzing voting patterns is well known. People vote their anxieties, their frustrations, their fears, occasionally their best selves. Yet one's religious self is always one's self, whether at best or worst.

American Jews were understandably alarmed at the mentality expressed by the Moral Majority during the 1980 presidential campaign. They had every reason to question the commitment of these zealots to the religious and cultural pluralism necessary if Jews are to survive. More alarming still was the lack of alarm shown by Catholics. There was little expression of dismay by Catholics at the silence of Catholic leadership during that period. An article in the *Washington Post* of March 8, 1981, by Senator Patrick Leahy (D., Vermont) recorded genuine distress at the desertion of the poor and the needy by Catholic voters and their religious leaders, lured as they were by various single-issue promises. Leahy maintained that this betrayal of what he had been taught was the Catholic Church's primary mission was a bad bargain: the doubtful benefits held out by political conservatives at the price of an unholy alliance with the radical right. More comfort for the comfortable, more misery for the miserable. Of such stuff an ancient tradition of prayer and praise in a setting of freedom is not made.

The essays in this collection wisely confine themselves to the areas of the essayists' expertise, which tend to be religious and historical. They are prescriptions, however, because their authors know the clear thrust of the traditions they represent. The biblical respect for the material, for the stark and undissolvable reality of God's creation, marks all of the contributions. Christianity's early flirtations with gnosticism and other dualisms are not reflected here. The tendency of the Hebrew Bible and its divergent commentaries — the Talmud and New Testament — is one of total respect for God's handiwork. Whatever *is* is not to be despised. Nature, all the earth's resources, are to be nurtured and fostered. When they prove a threat to human happiness they are to be curbed or controlled. The earth is the Lord's and the fullness thereof, but he is no miserly possessor. He gives with bounty. He expects the human creature in return to husband ingeniously and distribute justly.

A terrible responsibility is placed on the shoulders of the earth's one rational creature—namely, to cope with flood and earthquake, famine and fire, to provide for daily needs, and still produce a surplus for those less able to cope.

There is a tendency within humanity that resists this obligation. A downward pull exists, a selfish drive in every heart that would stop once the needs of the self have been fulfilled. The drive is deeply ingrained. Jews call it the *yetzer ha rah* and quickly point out that it is not an evil drive so much as the aggressive instinct that can lapse into injustice. It becomes evil only if it goes unchecked by the precepts of reason inculcated in the Torah. The Christian world knows the tendency as *epithymia* (in Latin, *concupiscentia*), the lasting fruit of the alienation known as original sin. Concupiscence is not merely desire but desire out of control, an inclination to satisfy any passion without respect to need or right. Reason can curb desire but only under the influence of grace, the divine assistance on which humanity must continually call.

It will not help to try to reconcile the Jewish and Christian views on the roots of evil: it probably cannot be done. The two are allied, however, in that both know the human race to be basically good yet mysteriously flawed. Humanity should be at peace with itself, yet it is not. It struggles, often unsuccessfully, to do what it should do and frequently does what it knows it should not do. To be human is to feel the pain of failure in right doing, to know the apathy of indifference toward one's fellow creatures. Both religious traditions require heeding the divine instruction if the human creature is not to slip into bestiality.

This moral imperative is deeply ingrained in biblical religion. No believers can claim the Hebrew scriptures as their own without acquiring obligations of stewardship toward the earth, toward fellow human beings, and especially toward the poor and needy. The biblical message is increasingly muted, however, in a secular society. Unlimited consumerism is proving to be its successful rival. The growth of populations that live in comfort, experiencing a surplus of goods and services, means the growth of corresponding populations that live below the poverty line. The first exist at the expense of the second, one might almost say in function of them. The poor are a by-product of the rich. A consequence of this is that any who are close enough to their religious tradition to assemble for prayer, however irregularly, must acquire there some awareness of the threat they pose to their neighbors' peace.

It is not only the comfortable who pray. But in today's society the stable members of congregations, Jewish and Catholic, tend to be not the poor but the middle and upper classes. They are part of the problem, not part of the solution. The acquisition at prayer of the sense of being an oppressor may seem to be a superhuman demand. Worshipers are already in a posture of gratitude or petition—a sense of fittingness at the very least—which sets them apart from their fellows. Is it further to be asked of them that they experience a sense of guilt for economic and social systems they never made, when complicity with these systems is often the only option open to them? Inwardly they may resist them, feel themselves victims as much as the poor, but at a higher level of helplessness. To place a new burden on the comfortable may be a gross insensitivity to the strains they already experience. Is there any way out of the dilemma of rich and poor who should be one society, one praying people, but who in fact are seldom found close to each other in religious circumstances?

There is a segment of the U.S. population that is glued to its radio Bible hour and the screen of the electronic church. It is anathema to another segment fixed to its benches or pews, listening stolidly and without emotion to earnest ethical messages. Occasionally there is song. A larger group than either of the two is scarcely if ever to be found in these formally religious circumstances except at birth, marriage, and death. Yet all have an idea of what they want out of life, and of what those who tell them what they ought to expect are getting out of life.

There is a vague but widespread awareness in the population of what Moses taught and what Jesus taught. There are strong convictions about what is fair and just and right. Sometimes the convictions are biblical and talmudic, sometimes they do not in the least accord with the teachings of the rabbis and the church fathers. But they are there, they are firmly in place. What the believing, praying people are being taught, the untempled and unchurched know almost by instinct. They may not be doing justice, but they are judging the pious in their piety, and the adverse judgments they make are usually not far from wrong.

The Jewish religious tradition is intensely ethical. It knows no God except a God of justice whose keen interest it is that all receive their due. With Christians it is the same. All claims on one side or the other of a stricter justice or a greater mercy (sometimes claims against the other) prove on close inspection to be false. The message about the attributes of deity is one and the same. A distinct possibility in both traditions is that the Holy One of Israel — Blessed be He — the one claimed to be "the Father of our Lord Jesus Christ," may be reduced to the dimensions of a petty moralist or a magistrate out to penalize unconscious offenders. There are all sorts of reasons why this is so. George Burns is winsome enough as an improvement on this God but he is painfully pallid after Sinai. He is probably the God we deserve, correcting mildly the mildly erroneous views we have of him. When it comes to unspeakable holiness — the God in whose presence the seraphs cover their eyes with their wings and cry, "Holy, Holy, Holy!" — the grandfatherly Burns in his baseball cap will not do. He is the classic nontheophany, indeed not even good Tolstoy. This segment of the American imagination derives ultimately not from Avery Korman or Hollywood but from the American pulpit and sanctuary. Burns should probably not be dismissed as the God we deserve. He is a cut above what we deserve.

A God of solely ethical concern, howsoever clement and understanding put in place of a God of inexpressible majesty, is no true God but a caricature. The precepts of Moses on Sinai are words of the Lord, a holy God, to his people. Christians see these words enunciated afresh in the sermon on the mount. In neither case are the ethical and ritual demands the sum total of religion. They make sense only in a setting of awe: eerie, unsettling otherness, the very godliness of God. This means that any efforts at worship that content themselves with the rational demands that a just God makes on his people are missing the mark. The God of Jews and Christians is totally awesome, un-conveyable in his elusive reality. The result of this uncomfortable fact is that logical presentations of the biblical rightness of ecology, to take one example, will move no one. The place for such appeals is the lecture hall. The same is true of exhortations to a more equitable social order embodying elemental economic justice. The convictions may be right but the setting is wrong. Sermons that are taken for lessons in politics are sermons that are not heard. But although all human life is intensely political — the lives of the religious and nonreligious alike — a people at prayer is not a people engaged in political activity. A people at prayer is to be invited, exhorted, commanded to the attitudes that stand behind all ethical and political choices.

Sabbath and Sunday services are potentially the medium of this communication. The thorny question of Hebrew and Latin as numinous tongues set aside, it remains true that the human voice in speech and song has an unrivaled power in conveying a range of moods and convictions. Bodily carriage, gesture, the slightest movement of participants in prayer are helpful in transmitting the demands of a transcendent order of reality. As to the texts of Bible and prayer books, sacramentary and lectionary, however one may rail at translations, these sources say great things in great ways. Handled with awe they become letters from heaven, powerful instruments of the holy presence. There are some grim strictures leveled at priest and prophet in Jeremiah 23 for their godless ways. Modern ministers of public prayer who preach and teach as part of such prayer would do well to attend:

> Thus says the Lord of hosts:
> Listen not to the words of your prophets,
> who fill you with emptiness;
> Visions of their own fancy they speak,
> not from the mouth of the Lord   [v. 16].

No commentary is needed. Filling the hearer with emptiness is a possibility in any communication. It can be compounded in the set and the formal. Sacred formulas in their solemnity lend themselves to stentorian tones, affected gravity. So delivered they become a caricature and can only be misheard. The opposite error is an informality that borders on chattiness, making *O God!* seem like the loftiest of communication. But these are lapses in manner, not in matter. Matter in this case is the designated texts of the day meditated on, prayed over, prepared for delivery—or, conversely, spoken perfunctorily at what is literally first sight.

A verse from Jeremiah 48 used to hang framed in the sacristy of the college chapel where I found myself in the mid-1930s. Later learning identified it as textually doubtful and contextually concerned with another matter, but its impact from youth onward has remained: "Cursed be he who does the work of the Lord negligently" (v. 10). For one trained in holy lore, to deal with the holy God casually can be the most serious sin. Indeed, the point comes early when lapses in manner are graver than those in matter, because we speak more tellingly with our bodies than with our words.

Romano Guardini, philosopher and liturgist, said at a meeting in Maine in 1964, which was concerned with public prayer, that there was a danger of allowing the necessary process of revising the texts and rites of Catholics to obscure the deeper issue. This he identified as "the problem of the cult act or, to be more precise, the liturgical act."[1] He pressed for "relearning a forgotten way of doing things" and "recapturing lost attitudes" rather than being content with removing anomalies that have crept into ancient rites or giving better instruction regarding them. Theology and *d'rash* are necessarily conceptual exercises. They are not to be minimized for what they alone can achieve. Yet a too conceptual understanding of forms of public prayer, including preaching, can lead to unrealistic expectations of the possibility of what are called in English "services." "Our problem," says Guardini, "is to rise above reading and writing and learn to look with understanding."[2]

Guardini was not a theologian or historian of public prayer forms. He was a classroom academic in philosophy who explored Western culture—biblical, Greek, and Christian—in various manifestations. No liturgiologist, he was a liturgist — that is, he practiced the art of leadership in prayer. A distinguished few of the contributors to this volume have the former expertise. All, however, are entrusted by church or synagogue with the latter responsibility. They have a corporate sense of the power of texts to convey the urgency of social justice to congregations. They are realistically familiar with the limitations of even inspired texts. The grace note this essay hopes to add to their impressive efforts is the reminder that great prayer is a responsibility of congregations and their leaders.

God has no need of prayer. People need it desperately. They need to rise above reading and writing, and learn to look with understanding. They have to understand the world they live in and the part they have in it. They must let the scales fall from their eyes and see what is there ("It is April, and I can see!"). Often what is there to be seen is a plundered earth and a victimized neighbor. Neither is in full view. Except for persons whose bellies are distended or whose limbs are bloody stumps, the victimization is not in full view. It must be identified, disclosed, acknowledged. That last is the most sensitive of all. The unconsciously disregarded, not the actively denied, is the last to come to light. Our culture is one of hidden hungers and glossed-over shames. The acknowledged injustice is the only one that can be dealt with.

"Consciousness-raising," a stuffy-sounding phrase like so many of our neologisms, nonetheless says much. It speaks of the reality of scales falling from the eyes of the mind. It describes the coming to sight of the emotionally and intellectually blind. For this to happen in congregational circumstances there must be great awe of the power of God, immense respect for the importance of the human person. The specific worship circumstances are not of consequence here. They may be a wedding, a funeral, or the regular weekly service. Every event is important to some, even if few are important to all. There cannot be peak experiences of emotion or intellect for many at once. That is not to be expected. But a high level of "learning to look with understanding," simply seeing what is there, is very much to be expected. "The most insidious and basic problem posed by the spirit of the age is . . . its 'flatminded literalism'."[3] Religious symbols are not allowed to flourish symbolically but are frozen into philosophical statements about God. "They do not configure and mobilize human experience, but are considered solely independent entities susceptible to a detached scrutiny."[4] Such use of language (or any other symbol) can rest forever on the plateau of literal understanding. It victimizes religious symbols into literal language designating invisible objects. It moves no one in any direction, simply falling on the ear (or any sense) as a tired cliché. The liturgist galvanizing readers, cantors, choir members, ushers, congregations must change all this. He or she is a choreographer of awe.

A people praying in awe can see and hear what others cannot see or hear about earthly realities. Theirs is an altered universe, a globe and its humanity changed. The possibility lies open to them of seeing for the first time the only creation that God has made.

One corollary needs to be added, not lamely, it is hoped, but firmly. When "spokesmen for the Jewish (or Catholic) community" — and, sadly, the gender specificity is correct — tell the press or congressional committees or public meetings what "the Catholic (or Jewish) view" is on this or that, they tend to do it neither better nor worse than the way they pray in the liturgies of their traditions. This does not say that a good ethicist must be a good liturgist; it says the reverse: a good liturgist *will be* a good ethicist, for in good liturgy the depths of the language of symbol have been plumbed. In the prayer of petition and praise, a holy God comes close to his people and moves them profoundly to do justice.

NOTES

1. From the Proceedings of the German Liturgical Congress in *Herder Correspondence* (August 1964), p. 237, quoted by Mark Searle, "Liturgy as Metaphor," *Worship*, 55 (March 1981), p. 99.

2. Guardini, "Proceedings," p. 238; Searle, "Liturgy," p. 100.

3. Searle, "Liturgy," p. 101.

4. John Shea, "The Second Naïveté: Approach to a Pastoral Problem," *Concilium*, 81 (1973), p. 110.

Contributors

Dr. Eugene J. Fisher
Executive Secretary, Secretariat for Catholic-Jewish Relations, National Conference of Catholic Bishops

Rev. John A. Gurrieri
Executive Director, Secretariat of the Bishops' Committee on the Liturgy, National Conference of Catholic Bishops

Rabbi Jules Harlow
The Rabbinical Assembly, New York

Dr. Jonathan I. Helfand
Professor of Judaic Studies, Brooklyn College, City University of New York

Rabbi Lawrence Hoffman
Professor of Liturgy, Hebrew Union College-Jewish Institute of Religion, New York

Rev. Edward J. Kilmartin, S.J.
Professor of Liturgy, University of Notre Dame

Rev. Dennis W. Krouse
Chairman, Department of Religious Studies, University of San Diego

Rev. John T. Pawlikowski, O.S.M.
Professor, Catholic Theological Union, Chicago

Rabbi Daniel F. Polish
Temple Israel, Los Angeles

Rev. Gerard S. Sloyan
Professor of Religion, Temple University, Philadelphia

Rabbi Walter S. Wurzburger
Congregation Shaaray Tefila, Lawrence, New York,
President, Synagogue Council of America